Managing Finance and Information

In Charge
Series Editor: Roger Cartwright

Managing People
Roger Cartwright, Michael Collins, George Green and Anita Candy

Managing Operations
Roger Cartwright, Michael Collins, George Green and Anita Candy

Managing Finance and Information
Roger Cartwright, Michael Collins, George Green and Anita Candy

NVQ/ SVQ LEVEL 3

Managing Finance and Information

A COMPETENCE APPROACH TO SUPERVISORY MANAGEMENT

IN CHARGE

Foreword from the MCI

Roger Cartwright • Michael Collins
George Green • Anita Candy

BLACKWELL
Business

First published 1993

Blackwell Publishers
108 Cowley Road
Oxford OX4 1JF
UK

238 Main Street
Cambridge, Massachusetts 02142
USA

British Library Cataloguing in Publication Data
A CIP catalogue record for this book is available from the British Library.

Library of Congress Cataloging-in-Publication Data has been applied for.

ISBN 0–631–190090
Typeset in 11.5 on 14 pt Palatino
by Joshua Associates Ltd, Oxford
Printed in Great Britain by
Page Bros, Norwich

Contents

List of Figures

Foreword

In pursuit of its strategy to improve the performance of UK organizations by improving the quality of their managers, MCI have developed competence-based management standards for practical use and as a basis for assessment for vocational awards.

In focusing at the supervisory management level, this book provides a simple and practical way of acquiring knowledge and understanding in preparation for the development of those standards, thus providing the first step in career progression for those aspiring to a managerial career.

The abundant case samples drawn from practical experience illustrate the elements of supervisory management activity which require achievement in most organizations. This book is heartily commended to all candidates seeking to develop such qualifications and offers a background to providers, employers and candidates to progress towards the achievement of their organization's objectives.

Vlad Stanić
Development Director
Management Charter Initiative

For June, Yvonne, Bronwen and Philip

We would like to express our grateful thanks to all those who have provided help and criticism during the preparation of the volumes of *In Charge*, especially to Blackwell Publishers and their reviewers – Donna Green of Rover Group, Jane Hawkins of NEBSM Regional Managers, Evelyn Lee-Barber of Bass plc, Sandy Milton of the Radcliffe Infirmary Oxford, and Terry Guy and Debbie Stones of Autotype International.

Jean walked out of the door trying to control her breathing. She hadn't known why Mr Raymond wanted to see her, although she didn't think that she'd done anything wrong.

When he offered her the vacant position of section supervisor (vacant because Jim had moved to the new offices) on a temporary basis pending the outcome of the current organizational review, she was filled with a mixture of thoughts:

The money would be useful

What about the responsibility?

What would the staff think?

How much extra time would it take?

She'd asked about Alan and Maureen who were both senior to her, but Mr Rawlings had said that Alan was taking up an offer of early retirement and Maureen wanted a job share that was on offer in another department.

She'd accepted the position but as she walked down the corridor one question above all others kept coming back into her mind:

'He's told me I'm going to be *In Charge* . . . but what does that actually mean?'

Introduction

This introduction to *Managing Finance and Information* is a summary of chapters 1–3 of *In Charge* volume 1, *Managing People*.

- What the series is about
- Who the series is intended for
- Programmes for which the volumes will be useful
- Scope of the volumes
- How to use the volumes
- Supervisors and managers – what's in a title?
- What is management competence?
- The management standards
- Demonstrating competence
- Competence audit
- Personal competences

WHAT THE SERIES IS ABOUT

The three volumes in this series are designed to provide those in supervisory and first line management positions with the knowledge and skills to carry out their supervisory and management tasks with competence.

WHO THE SERIES IS INTENDED FOR

If you have responsibilities for others within your organization or you are seeking such responsibility, you will find this series useful. You may have been in your post for some time, you may have been promoted recently or you may be seeking promotion: in all these cases, this series will provide you with useful knowledge and understanding to support you within the work situation and will aid you with your managerial/supervisory and personal development.

The series is intended to be equally relevant to all areas of work and contains cases from the private, public and voluntary sectors.

The series will also provide useful material for those responsible for training at the level of, and has been specially designed to support National Vocational Qualification (NVQ) or Scottish Vocational Qualification (SVQ) programmes at Level 3 supervisory management.

PROGRAMMES FOR WHICH THE VOLUMES WILL BE USEFUL

In Charge has been written to support supervisory/first line management development programmes at NVQ or SVQ Level 3 in addition to company short courses and individual development.

Such courses, validated by BTEC, ISM and NEBSM, are offered by large numbers of further education establishments and by open learning providers.

SCOPE OF THE VOLUMES

The areas covered are:

Volume 1 *Managing People*

This volume commences by looking at how ideas of supervision and management have developed over time and then considers how to manage people effectively. It covers: motivation; human reactions to change; recruitment, selection and training; working with teams and groups; leadership; handling conflict; and concludes with a consideration of the role of the supervisor/first line manager in the discipline and grievance process.

Volume 2 *Managing Operations*

This volume looks at the operations of an organization and the part played by supervisors and junior managers. The volume examines the different types of organizations you will encounter (public sector, private sector etc.) and considers the relationship between operations and other organizational functions (marketing, personnel etc.). The volume then examines the operations function in more detail, covering both work practices, planning, resourcing, legislation (e.g. HSAW) and customer relations.

Volume 3 *Managing Finance and Information*

This volume covers two key areas of supervision and first line management. Managing information examines the types of information the supervisor/first line manager is likely to encounter, and considers ways of disseminating and presenting such information. The finance section is designed to give the reader a broad overview of the role finance plays in an organization; it is not intended to turn the reader into an accountant, but rather to provide the supervisor/first line manager with an understanding of financial language and practices as they relate to the work situation.

HOW TO USE THE VOLUMES

No set of books, however well written, can provide the answer to a specific problem that an individual has encountered. However, by providing the individual with an insight into the processes that are at work within situations, and with opportunities to examine situations from a variety of standpoints, books such as those in the *In Charge* series can allow the supervisor/first line manager to make more informed decisions.

Use the volumes as you would a handbook: scan through first to gain the flavour of the subject and then you can home in on specifics. The volumes form an integrated package, and while each can stand alone, at the same time they support each other and refer you backwards and forwards. Supervision and first line management tasks cannot be pigeon-holed into purely managing people or solely managing finance, and neither can an effective supporting text.

SUPERVISORS AND MANAGERS – WHAT'S IN A TITLE?

Supervisor	Foreman
Chargehand	Senior ....
First Line Manager	NCO (Armed Forces)
Junior Manager	Assistant Manager
Trainee Manager	Team Leader
Coordinator	Administrator
Section Leader	Staff Nurse

Organizations within the United Kingdom display little consistency in the titles given to those working in supervisory/junior management positions. One company may consider a person to be a supervisor while another company may designate a similar post 'assistant manager'; it all depends on the type of company, the way in which positions have evolved, and industry custom and practice.

WHAT IS MANAGEMENT COMPETENCE?

The Concise Oxford Dictionary defines 'competent' as:

(a) adequately qualified or capable
(b) effective

How does one judge effectiveness or capability? The traditional approach to management/supervisory development was based upon standardized inputs: a set course of study, knowledge workshops etc., followed by some form of away-from-work examination. This form of development was able to test how much the participant had understood the concepts but was unable to test for them in actual work situations.

A competence approach uses evidence gained either from the work place or from work related simulations to measure the effectiveness not of the learning but of the actual participant. To accomplish this requires a set of national standards against which competence can be measured.

A good example of a competence approach is the driving test. The examiner judges each person against a set of national criteria. How a person learned to drive is unimportant: the test measures whether they are a competent driver on the day.

However, to drive competently requires more than just undertaking a short test, it also requires knowledge and understanding (hence the Highway Code test). People taking their test do not normally do so using the exact right turns, parking exercises etc. that they practised on. They need the understanding necessary to transfer from practice exercises to those on the test.

THE MANAGEMENT STANDARDS

The competence of a supervisor or manager can be measured against national standards, like those in the case of a driving test.

The Management Charter Initiative (MCI) is the lead body for developing management standards in the United Kingdom. At the time of writing (1993), standards have been developed at 3 levels:

M2	(NVQ/SVQ5)	for more senior managers
M1	(NVQ/SVQ4)	for junior/middle managers
M1 (Subset)	(NVQ/SVQ3)	for supervisors/first line managers

The standards allow a person to judge their competence in an objective manner by seeing how their performance matches up to the national criteria.

Because the standards are based more on what a person does than on what they know, they are of equal use to those undertaking a course of study and those who only wish to know more about their own effectiveness.

The standards are arranged in 4 key role areas:

Managing People
Managing Operations
Managing Information
Managing Finance

The supervisory standards include a limited consideration of the management of finance within the operations role, as it is appreciated that supervisors/first line managers may have little day-to-day contact with the finance functions. Finance is included within the *In Charge* series in its own right, in the present volume, because it is believed that those entering supervision and management will need a fuller appreciation of the role finance plays within their organization.

Each key role area is divided into a number of units which are further divided into elements of competence. See figure 0.1, a diagram of the Supervisory Management Standards produced by the MCI.

The elements contain a series of performance criteria and range statements relating to that element. Performance criteria specify the outcomes a competent supervisor/first line manager should achieve and range statements describe the circumstances within which the element is applied. These criteria and statements will be readily available to those who need them for the production of evidence as part of a formal qualification. One example is reproduced below.

Unit 1 Maintain services and operations to meet quality standards	Element 1.1 Maintain services and operations
	Element 1.2 Maintain the necessary conditions for an effective and safe work environment
Unit 2 Contribute to the planning, monitoring and control of resources	Element 2.1 Plan for the use of resources
	Element 2.2 Monitor and control the use of resources
Unit 3 Contribute to the provision of personnel	Element 3.1 Contribute to the identification of personnel requirements
	Element 3.2 Contribute to the selection of personnel
Unit 4 Contribute to the training and development of teams, individuals and self to enhance performance	Element 4.1 Contribute to planning the training and development of teams and individuals
	Element 4.2 Contribute to training and development activities for teams and individuals
	Element 4.3 Contribute to the assessment of teams and individuals against training and development objectives
	Element 4.4 Develop oneself within the job

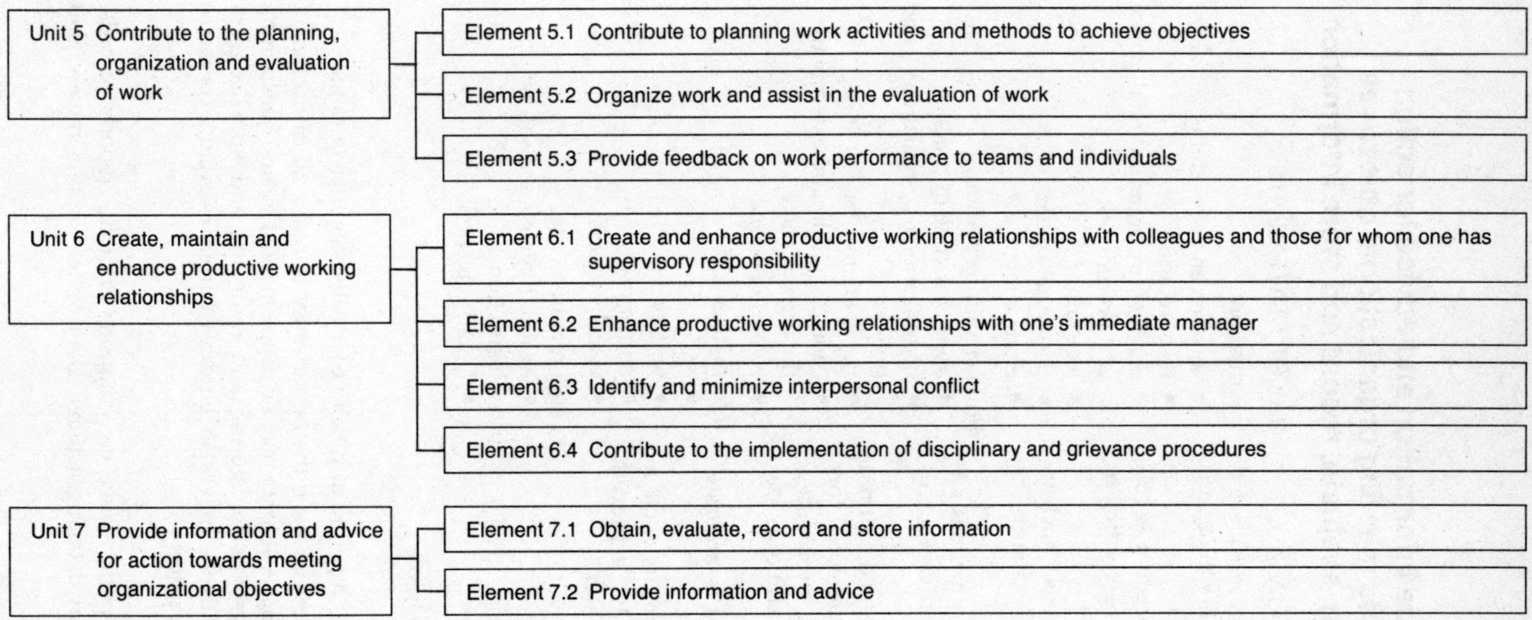

Figure 0.1 Structure of supervisory management standards
Permission from MCI.

Unit 7 Provide information and advice for action towards meeting organizational objectives

Element 7.1 Obtain, evaluate, record and store information

PERFORMANCE CRITERIA

(a) Specified information is collected and up-dated according to organizational requirements
(b) Other relevant information is collected and dealt with according to its nature and content
(c) Where information is unclear, clarification and assistance is obtained
(d) Inadequacies in information are identified and alternative sources are sought
(e) Information is recorded, stored and retrieved using accepted formats, systems and procedures, according to organizational requirements
(f) Information recorded is accurate, complete and legible
(g) Information is stored in such a way that it can be retrieved promptly when required

RANGE STATEMENTS

Information:

- services and operations
- resourcing
- changes in organizational policy and procedures
- legislation
- personnel issues
- environment

Sources of information:

- approved code of practice
- organizational regulations and policies
- publications
- contacts within and external to the organization
- computer-based

Information is:

- oral
- written
- numerical
- visual/pictorial

Legal requirements:

- health, hygiene and safety legislation
- Data Protection Act

EVIDENCE SPECIFICATIONS

Sources of Evidence:

Performance at work over a period of time to cover all categories of range.

Where the candidate does not have the opportunity to cover all categories of range within the work place, evidence may be supplemented by oral questioning for understanding of systems for storing and retrieving and knowledge of information sources. Evidence may also be drawn from relevant experience outside the current work place.

Forms of Evidence:

Outputs and products of performance, e.g. computer printouts, reports, records, diagrams, personal report detailing actions taken, reflection and review, and planning.

DEMONSTRATING COMPETENCE

How do you demonstrate competence? In the main you can only demonstrate that you are competent at a task by carrying out that task to a defined standard. The *In Charge* series is designed around the Supervisory Management Standards.

There are only two states attached to competence:

Competent – having provided sufficient evidence of competency
Not yet competent – having provided insufficient evidence of competence

Those in the latter category are working towards competence.

An important feature of the Management Standards is their applicability across jobs. The same standards apply in public, private and voluntary sector firms and organizations. The tasks and context of the tasks change but the managerial competences remain as a constant.

Each volume of *In Charge* commences with a 'competence audit' to allow the reader to assess what it is they do and their competence at it based on the National Standards. The competence audit asks you to look at each element of the Management Standards and to consider whether you do that task in your current job, or have done it in a previous job, and how competent you feel you really are.

You should now examine and complete the competence audit for managing information reproduced in figure 0.2.

Unit/Element	Do I do this in my job?			Have I ever done this in a job?			How competent do I feel I am?		
	O	S	N	O	S	N	V	P	N
7 Provide information and advice for action towards meeting organizational objectives									
7.1 Obtain, evaluate, record and store information									
7.2 Provide information and advice									

For task: O = often S = sometimes N = never
For competency: V = very P = partially N = not very

Figure 0.2 The Managing Information Competence Audit

PERSONAL COMPETENCES

The competence standards we have looked at relate to the functions the supervisor/first line manager carries out. They can be considered as **functional competences**, i.e., as directly related to the job the supervisor/first line manager does. There are also a set of competences that relate to the personal attributes needed to be a competent manager at any level, ranging from supervisor to senior manager. These are known as **personal competences**.

The *In Charge* series covers both functional and personal competences. Each volume contains information on the personal competences and the functional competences to which they are linked.

Section I
Managing Finance

In this section we are going to take a broad overview of the role finance plays in an organization. It is not intended to turn you into an accountant, but will provide you with a working knowledge of the language used by those in the finance function.

Although the management standards for first line managers and supervisors make little mention of finance, the writers of the *In Charge* series believe that such a working knowledge of financial matters will underpin competency in other key role areas.

Some of the subjects covered in this section – such as balance sheets and profit and loss accounts in chapter 2, and the cashflow forecasts in chapter 3 – may appear to have little or nothing to do with most first line managers and supervisors. These subjects will, however, make some of the decisions taken by senior management more understandable and, for example, explain why additional business must at times be turned down, or why new machinery and equipment cannot be purchased. This understanding should help us also to find ways of becoming more effective in our jobs. We all like to think that we are efficient in what we do, but efficiency is the relationship between the effort and resources that are put into something, and the results created by it. Effectiveness, by comparison, concentrates solely on the achievement of required results perhaps through finding new or different ways of doing a job.

The section contains a case study based on a plumbing business. The founder is made redundant and sets up on a self-employed basis. We then follow the progress of the business as it grows and becomes, first, a partnership, and then a limited company, eventually reaching the point where the work has to be divided up with different people taking responsibility for each of the areas. We have chosen this approach because it is easier to see the overall picture of a business first, and then how the part for which we are personally responsible fits into the whole.

Chapter 1

Understanding Businesses

In this chapter we are going to look at the various types of businesses and organizations for which we all work. This may seem strange in a book on finance, but all of these bodies receive and spend money. The ways in which they do so often vary according to their size and structure, so an understanding of the basic differences between them will help us later on.

It does not matter whether you are a supervisor/first line manager in charge of a shop, a team, a department, a process, an office, a shift or some other unit: it will usually be part of a larger concern. However, exceptions to this would be running your own business or running a business for the owner. So we will look first at the smallest and simplest of businesses.

THE SOLE TRADER

A sole trader is a business where one person is in business on their own. He or she provides the capital, owns the profit and is responsible for any debts resulting from losses. Whilst the term suggests that they are 'one-person businesses', this is not necessarily the case. The business is owned by one person but may employ a number of people.

There are a huge number of businesses of this type. Obvious examples include shopkeepers, farmers, plumbers, electricians etc.

The advantages of this type of business include:

1. They are simple to set up.
2. The capital required to start the business may be quite small.
3. The owner can keep his or her business interests confidential as they are not required to publish their results except to the Inland Revenue.

4 The business, because of its size, is usually very flexible, and the owner can adapt it to changes in the market quite quickly.
5 The owner, in most cases, is able to completely change the goods and services offered without legal formality.
6 Because the business is usually small the owner is in touch with everything that is going on.

The main disadvantages of this type of business include:

1 The owner is personally responsible for all of the debts of the business. In the event of a business failure the owner could lose all of his/her personal money and property, and be made bankrupt.
2 There is likely to be a lack of capital to invest in machinery, buildings etc.
3 It can be more difficult to borrow money for capital items or stock, materials etc.
4 The business must usually depend on all-round knowledge and expertise of the owner as professional advice can be too expensive.
5 Many owners are more comfortable carrying out their trade or business and neglect the bookkeeping – sending out invoices for work done, V.A.T. returns etc., with disastrous results.
6 The small size of this sort of business means that it is unable to compete on price with the bulk buying arrangements of its larger competitors.

If this type of business continues to grow there will come a time when it will need to change to a different legal form.

THINK POINT

Make a list of some of the sole traders you know who operate in very different trades and businesses.

Case Note 1

When Colin Wells was made redundant he decided to use his redundancy payment and savings to set up in business as a plumber, working from home. To start the business he needed a van, tools and a basic stock of materials. As he completed jobs he found that he also needed money to tide him over until customers settled their bills – although he found that this was partly offset by having a credit account with the company where he bought his materials.

This is the basis of most new small businesses. An adequate sum of money is required to buy the necessities for the business, finance the delay before customers pay and have enough on which to live until the business is making enough money to pay a reasonable wage.

THE PARTNERSHIP

A partnership is defined by the Partnership Act of 1890 as 'the relation which subsists between persons carrying on a business in common with a view to profit'. If we look behind this piece of typically legalistic writing we find that a partnership is made up of two or more people who are in business together.

Very often in setting up a partnership the people concerned get a solicitor to draw up a legal agreement which they then sign. This sets out certain ground rules which will govern how profits will be shared, what will happen to the property or assets of the partnership if one partner dies or if they fall out etc.

Where there is no partnership agreement the provisions of the Partnership Act will apply.

Most partnerships are quite small and are limited by law to no more than twenty partners. However, certain professions such as solicitors, accountants and stockbrokers are exempted from this, and as a result some accountancy partnerships are very large.

Like sole traders most partnerships are quite small, although there is a greater tendency for them to have employees.

The advantages of this type of business include:

1 They are simple to set up.
2 The capital required to start the business may be quite small and is probably more available than in a sole trader business.
3 The partners can keep their business interests confidential as they are not required to publish their results except to the Inland Revenue.
4 The business, because of its size, is usually very flexible, and the owner can adapt it to changes in the market quite quickly.

5 The partners, in most cases, are able to completely change the goods and services offered without legal formality.
6 The knowledge and expertise is likely to be greater than in a sole trader business.
7 The management and administration can be shared.

The main disadvantages of this type of business include:

1 Each partner is personally liable for all of the debts of the business, even though they might have been caused by the incompetence or dishonesty of their other partner(s).
2 The small size of this sort of business means that they are unable to compete on price with the bulk buying arrangements of their larger competitors.
3 If partners fall out it is possible that they will have to wind up or divide the business as a result.
4 In the event of the death, bankruptcy or lunacy of one partner, the partnership would have to be dissolved – unless this event is allowed for in the partnership agreement.

Most trading partnerships tend to have only two or three partners, and many of these partnerships are family businesses. With the exception of professional firms, as soon as a partnership grows to require more than three partners the benefits of limited liability, as offered by limited company status, tend to look very attractive, even though it means losing some advantages.

THINK POINT

Make a list of partnerships that you know, and have a look in the Yellow Pages to see which professions, trades and industries tend to have partnerships. These are likely to be printed in the form 'Messrs Smith and Jones', 'John Smith & Son' or 'Jones Bros'. Many entries will be in a trade name, such as 'Crossroads Garage' or 'Flower Power', and in these cases you will not be able to tell whether they are owned by sole traders, partnerships or limited companies.

Case Note 2

By the time Colin Wells had been in business as a sole trader for two years he found that he had more work than he could handle on his own. He was considering taking on an assistant when his brother, Jack, who worked as a plumber for one of the large building contractors, was also made redundant. As the two brothers had always got on very well together they decided to go into partnership. They had the solicitor, who had acted for Colin and his wife when they bought their house, draw up a partnership agreement for them. Jack used his redundancy money and some savings to buy another van and tools and to match the amount of money that Colin had built up in the business.

LIMITED COMPANIES

Limited liability companies are formed very differently from sole traders and partnership businesses. They have to be created within a strict legal framework because they have an identity of their own which is quite separate from that of their owners. Just in the same way as an individual can own property and goods in his or her own name or be sued in court, so can a limited company. A person at birth has to be registered and the parents receive the birth certificate. In a similar way a company at its incorporation must be registered, and the company secretary will receive a certificate of incorporation.

The most important feature of a limited company is that in the event of a business failure the owners or shareholders of such a company are only required to pay the company's debts to the nominal value of their shares in that company.

As that sounds very legalistic, let us look at an example by continuing with our case study.

Case Note 3

After a further year of successful trading the Wells brothers decided that it was time to take on additional help and to recognize the work that their wives had done in the office, collecting and delivering materials etc., and the part-time help with the plumbing work by Jack's wife, Karen, who was newly qualified. They also wanted to make sure that if anything should happen to the business which resulted in it failing they would not lose their houses, furniture and any personal savings. They therefore went to see their solicitor to arrange to set up a limited company to be called Wells (Plumbers) Limited. The brothers and their wives were to be the four directors of the company and each would own 25 per cent of the shares. The nominal share capital was agreed at £20,000, made up of 20,000 £1 shares. This meant that each of the four directors owned shares with a nominal value of £5,000, and this, in the event of the company going into liquidation, would be the extent of their liability.

There are actually two sorts of limited liability companies.

The first is a **public limited company**. This is a company which has been registered as a public limited company under the Companies Act of 1985 and can therefore invite members of the public to buy its shares. These companies can easily be identified by the letters 'plc' after their names. They will usually be large companies and, although at present they must have a share capital of at least £50,000, most plcs would have share capital of many millions of pounds.

Public limited companies account for approximately 80 per cent of all business in the UK, but this figure excludes the turnover of the remaining nationalized industries.

The main advantages of a public liability company are:

1 In the event of the company failing the shareholders are limited to the loss of the nominal value of their shares.
2 The shares are easily transferable when sold.
3 Many of the public limited companies have their shares traded on the stock-markets, which encourages wider share ownership.
4 Because of their size, reputation and the fact that their accounts are available for public inspection, plcs are able to raise additional capital far more easily.
5 They are usually able to raise loans and arrange overdraft facilities more easily and to pay lower rates for these monies on the grounds of their reputation and wealth.

The main disadvantages of a public liability company are:

1 Because of the requirements to publish their accounts, their affairs are discussed in the press and their actions and results are open to criticism. This can result in plcs looking for short-

term gains in order to keep the stock-market happy rather than investing for long-term growth.

2 The availability of the shares on the stock-market and the wide share ownership can make them the target for a takeover bid by another company, or even an individual.

3 The costs of setting up a plc and producing and sending out the balance sheets and accounts to all of the shareholders can be very high.

The second sort of limited liability company is referred to as a **private limited company**. These cover nearly all other companies which do not satisfy the requirements of the Companies Act of 1985 to be public limited companies. In this case they will have the familiar 'Ltd' after their names.

Like plcs they have the advantage of limited liability for the shareholders in the event of failure. They cannot, however, raise additional capital from the general public. Also, because they are usually much smaller, their limited liability status can make banks and finance houses reluctant to lend to them without adequate security.

We have so far looked at three main types of trading organizations, but it is quite possible that your employer will not be amongst them. So let us now look at some of the other major employers in the UK.

NATIONAL AND LOCAL GOVERNMENT

This is a huge area of employment, ranging from national government departments responsible for Health, Defence, Social Security, Education etc., and County Councils and Metropolitan Borough Councils with responsibility for schools, the police force, fire services etc., to City and District Councils who look after refuse collection, local planning, council houses and so forth. Each of these departments and authorities is controlled by laws and/or rules and is audited to ensure that they are adhered to. In certain instances local councillors can be held personally financially liable for their decisions.

NATIONALIZED INDUSTRIES

Whilst this area has been very much reduced by privatization it still represents a substantial area in terms of employment and spending power. Strictly speaking, nationalized industries are those public corporations which are mainly involved in industry and trading activities. These would obviously include the Post Office and British Coal. There are, however, other public organizations which do not fit this definition but which we tend to regard as nationalized industries rather than parts of government departments. Examples of these would be the Bank of England, the Forestry Commission and Ordnance Survey.

Other organizations include religious bodies, charities, cooperatives, friendly societies and trade associations. Each of these will have their own rules; many have special legal status which often involves further rules specifying how their finances must be controlled.

There will always be changes in the status of these organizations and the movement of work between the public and private sectors. Further privatization, trust status for hospitals, schools leaving the state education system, colleges of further education becoming incorporated and many more such changes will play a part. However, whatever changes take place, supervisors and managers at all levels will still have a responsibility to make the money work as effectively as possible. The following chapters are designed to help us in that task.

THINK POINT

In what sort of organization do you work?

SUMMARY

In this chapter we have looked at the various types of businesses and organizations:

- the sole trader
- the partnership
- the limited company
- local and national government
- nationalized industries

In addition we have met Colin, Sue, Jack and Karen Wells, who we shall be following throughout this book.

Chapter 2

Keeping Track of the Money

Supervisory Management Standards	
Unit 2	Contribute to the planning, monitoring and control of resources
Element 2.2	Monitor and control the use of resources
Unit 7	Provide information and advice for action towards meeting organizational objectives
Element 7.1	Obtain, evaluate, record and store information

The title of this chapter appears to be a very simple one, and an exercise which the majority of us have to practise in our private lives in order to make ends meet. Really it is what bookkeeping and accounting are all about, but most of us tend to 'glaze over' at the thought of them. The reason for this reaction in us is that unless we work in the accounts department and therefore have some 'hands-on' experience, the procedures and the terms used can be very off-putting. They tend to remind us of those school maths lessons that we did not understand. However, if we gain a little knowledge and understanding of the subject it can be seen that it is all based on a set of simple common-sense ideas.

When Colin Wells set up in business as a plumber we learned that he used his redundancy payment and savings to buy a van, tools and a basic stock of materials. He needed money to live on and to buy more materials whilst he waited for customers to pay their bills. He also owed money to his suppliers. In these circumstances we would all recognize the need to keep our personal money separate from the business, and so would pay ourselves a wage or salary from the business. We would also all see the need to keep some records so that we knew how we were doing, how much customers owed us, and how much we owed to our suppliers.

We have just identified three of the main reasons why businesses need to keep books and accounts:

1 To see whether or not the business is trading profitably
2 To calculate how much money they owe to others
3 To calculate how much money they are owed and by whom

In addition to the three reasons listed above there are also statutory requirements for maintaining accurate books and accounts. The Inland Revenue need to be able to calculate how much tax is owing and be satisfied that the figures are correct. Sole traders and partners have to pay income tax on the profits, whereas limited companies pay corporation tax.

H.M. Customs and Excise require accurate bookkeeping by businesses that are registered for V.A.T. (Value Added Tax) and their inspectors carry out spot checks to ensure that the tax returns are correct. (They also have the right to investigate businesses which are not registered for V.A.T. but should be.)

With regard to limited companies, both public and private limited companies are bound by law to make an annual report to their shareholders and to file a copy with the Registrar of Companies. Here the law specifies how the 'profit and loss account' and 'balance sheet' should be set out.

When Colin Wells started off in business his wife, Sue, agreed to look after all the paperwork so that he could concentrate on obtaining and doing the plumbing work. Sue had only ever kept a cash book before, so she went on a one-day course (organized by their local Training and Enterprise Council) to learn about bookkeeping in small businesses. On the course she learned about double entry bookkeeping and decided that she would operate the books in this way, although many small businesses operate on a simple cash book system.

Most of us do not need to know how to do bookkeeping and the following short section is included so that we understand what is involved. More importantly, it is intended to clear up a basic misconception that most of us have about 'credit' balances and 'debit', or overdrawn, balances.

DOUBLE ENTRY BOOKKEEPING

We called this chapter 'Keeping Track of the Money', and this is what double entry bookkeeping is all about, as money comes into and goes out of the business. Each transaction or movement of money has two aspects. One is the increase or decrease in the money or cash within the business; the other concerns the goods or services bought or sold by that sum of money. The double entry nature of our accounting enables us to record both these aspects of each transaction.

For example, when Colin put his redundancy money and savings of £10,000 in to start the business, Sue recorded the fact by showing that the business bank account had £10,000 in it and also that the business now owed Colin £10,000 in his personal capacity. Obviously this was intended to keep Colin's personal affairs separate from the business.

Another example would be when Colin went to the wholesalers for copper piping and some other materials. As he had opened an account with the wholesalers he received the goods on credit and they sent him a statement at the end of the month. Each time Colin went to the wholesalers he received an invoice which Sue entered in the books under the name of the supplier as money owed by the business. She also made an entry under 'purchases' to record the fact that materials had been bought for re-sale to customers. When she received a statement at the end of the month from the wholesalers Sue checked the details against the invoices and then sent a cheque to the wholesalers for the total of the invoices for that month. This she recorded against the bank account record and against the account of the supplier.

To make sense of whether it is money owing to the business or money owed by the business we rule a line down the centre of the page and enter the transactions on the different sides. We enter debits on the left and credits on the right.

The words *debit* and *credit* do not mean exactly the same in bookkeeping as they do in everyday usage. Debit means to receive or value received, and credit means to give or value given. So in bookkeeping we have to decide:

- for a debit, which account should receive this amount or which account should be debited, and
- for a credit, which account should give this amount or which account should be credited.

This appears to be the opposite from our past experience. Because few of us have had our own books we have always had our balances expressed from the other person's point of view. When we have money in the bank we receive a bank statement which shows that we are in 'credit', and when we receive a statement from someone we owe money to it shows that we are in 'debit' to them. This is because the statements are copies of their bookkeeping and are seen from their point of view and not ours. To the bank the 'credit' balance on our account shows that they owe us the money, whereas in our books, if we kept them, it would show as a 'debit' because the bank owes us the money.

Let's have a look at what Sue's books showed at this point (see figure 2.1). So far there have only been a very few transactions. The money that Colin put in to start the business is shown as his capital and the other part of the transaction is the entry in the bank account. The purchases from and payments to his suppliers, Plumber Supplies Ltd, are shown. Sue had to abbreviate Plumber Supplies Ltd to Plumber Supps Ltd in some places.

If we balanced off the four accounts at this point – i.e., added up both sides of each account and took one from the other – we would find that the balances would be those shown opposite.

Colin Wells Capital Account

	£		£
		Apl 1 Cash	10,000

Bank Account

Apl 1 C. Wells Capital	10,000	Apl 30 Plumber Supps Ltd	550

Plumber Supplies Ltd

Apl 30 Bank Acc	550	Apl 3 Purchases Inv. 902	275
		Apl 10 Purchases Inv. 1103	150
		Apl 17 Purchases Inv. 1321	125

Purchases Account

Apl 3 Plumber Supps Ltd	275		
Apl 10 Plumber Supps Ltd	150		
Apl 17 Plumber Supps Ltd	125		

Figure 2.1 Colin Wells' accounts

	£ Dr	£ Cr
Colin Wells Capital Account		10,000
Bank Account	9,450	
Plumbers Supplies Ltd Account		nil
Purchases Account	550	
Totals	10,000	10,000

Because Sue had entered each transaction twice and on different sides, the two sides balance.

We must always remember that every debit entry must have a credit one, and vice versa.

The list of balances that we made from Sue's accounts is referred to as a 'trial balance' and is the point where the accountant takes over from the bookkeeper. The bookkeeper enters the transactions from the documents he or she is given, while the accountant has to interpret them, make decisions and provide information.

MONEY COMES INTO A BUSINESS FROM:

Capital and loan capital

We have now looked at how the various transactions would be recorded to enable us to keep track of the money in the business. So far we have seen how Colin started his business by putting in his own money from his redundancy payment and from savings. This we have referred to as his 'Capital'. As an alternative to putting in all the capital himself he could have borrowed some on a long-term basis from a relation or bank etc. This loan would have been entered as a separate account in the books and would be known as 'loan capital'. (In the case of a bank or other professional lender, they would almost certainly have required some form of security, such as a mortgage on his house.)

We have now learned that when starting up a business there are two places that money can come from:

1 The owner. We call this his or her 'capital' or, in the case of a limited company, the 'share capital', as the people who put up

the money receive 'shares' in the company and are known as 'shareholders'.

2 Money borrowed on a long-term basis for use in the business. This is called 'loan capital'.

At the end of Colin's first year of trading, Sue balanced all of the accounts and then listed the resulting debit and credit balances so that they agreed. She then drew up a 'trading and profit and loss statement' for the year to calculate what profit had been made. This gave a third way in which money comes into a business – retained profits, which are referred to as 'reserves'.

Reserves

Retained profits or reserves are the most common way that businesses finance their growth, and they need these in times of inflation – which nowadays is all the time – just to stand still! It is usually not possible for the owners of small businesses to put in more capital, and shareholders of public companies are often reluctant to do so unless it is for expansion and increased profits look certain. Loan capital can be expensive, as the lender will want a rate of return that makes it worthwhile. There is little point in risking your money by lending to a business if you can get almost as good a rate of return by leaving it safely in a building society account. Retained profits are by far the cheapest and most desirable way of financing the future growth and development of any business.

MONEY GOES OUT OF A BUSINESS TO:

In the case of Colin Wells we have seen that there are two main areas where money can go out:

1 *Fixed Assets* We saw that when Colin was starting the business he needed to buy certain things to keep in the business and use for his work. These included his van and tools. Such items are known as 'fixed assets', and could also include buildings, machinery, furniture and fittings etc.

2 *Working Capital* Colin also needed money for the day-to-day working of the business. He needed to buy materials, have cash available, pay wages to himself and his wife, allow time

for customers to pay him for work done and pay other bills such as electricity and petrol. This group is referred to as 'working capital', but they are not all payments out (note we have included the money owed to him by customers, the balance in his bank account and any petty cash). So some of these amounts are used to offset the amounts that go out.

Working capital

Working capital is the name given to the excess of the total of current assets, over the total of current liabilities.

Current assets

We learned earlier that fixed assets is the name we give to those major items a business buys to keep to use, such as its buildings, machines, motor vehicles, furniture and fittings, tools etc. The items that a business buys eventually to sell – such as copper pipe, washers, radiators etc. in Colin's case – are referred to as 'current assets'. Current, because they are always changing. Also included in current assets are cash, bank balances and the money owed to the business by customers for work done. All of these items are capable eventually of becoming cash or money in the bank.

The stocks of materials would be used by Colin on customers' jobs. The customers would then owe money to Colin and would therefore have become debtors. The debtors would pay Colin the money they owe and he would be back with cash or money in the bank.

Current liabilities

Liabilities is the name given to the amounts of money that the business owes, which are the amounts the business is liable to pay. We mentioned long-term loans when we discussed loan capital, and these would obviously be long-term liabilities. Current liabilities are similar to current assets in that they are always changing. They represent money that the business owes for goods and services used in what it is going to sell. Examples would include the amounts that it owes to its suppliers for materials or stock, the electricity bill it has not yet paid, a bank overdraft.

Below we have used the term 'Creditors' to indicate those people to whom Colin owes money for materials and other costs like electricity, petrol etc.; and 'Debtors' for those customers who had been invoiced by Sue and have not yet paid up.

Working Capital

Current Assets:			
Materials	600		
Debtors	1,000		
Bank	1,500		
Cash	150	3,250	
Less Current Liabilities:			
Creditors	1,150	1,150	
			2,100

We can see that in this example Colin's amount of working capital was £2,100. In a later chapter we shall be looking at the importance of controlling the amount of money we have tied up in working capital to ensure that it is adequate and that it is being used efficiently.

Investments

So far we have seen two main areas that money can go out to, fixed assets and working capital. One further place is investments. There are two main ways in which this is done. The first is where the business has surplus cash available for a time and puts the money in a building society, bank deposit account or similar investment to gain interest. The second is where it invests or buys shares in another trading business. This might be in a major supplier or customer to strengthen the business relationship.

Obviously it was much too early for Colin to consider buying shares in another business. He might, however, have found that he did not need to use all of his £10,000 in the business straight away, and could invest some in a building society to earn interest until he required it.

So far we have introduced a number of the words used by accountants:

- purchases
- capital

- share capital
- loan capital
- fixed assets
- working capital
- liabilities
- current assets
- current liabilities
- creditors
- debtors
- investments

These give us a language so that when we refer to such items others who are also 'in the know' will understand us. If you are uncertain of the meanings of any of the above this would be a good time to check up on them, either by looking back to where we have used them or by reference to the glossary at the end of the book.

Sue's calculations at the end of Colin's first year are shown in exhibit 2.1.

Exhibit 2.1 Trial balance

	Debits	Credits
Capital		10,000
Bank Current Account	1,100	
Building Society Account	3,000	
Cash	200	
Van	6,000	
Tools	800	
Purchases	22,000	
Sales		40,000
Motor Expenses	1,700	
Part-time wages (to Sue)	1,500	
Office costs	200	
Plumber Supplies Ltd		700
Sundry debtors	2,200	
Drawings (Colin's wages)	12,000	
Totals	50,700	50,700

As we saw earlier in the chapter, the 'trial balance' is simply a list of the outstanding balances of all of the accounts in our double entry bookkeeping system which, if properly maintained, should balance. There is no need to worry about the fact that some of the balances are in credit while others appear as debits: this is the conventional way of entering them. Let us just accept that where the business owes money it is shown as a credit – e.g., it owed £700 to Plumber Supplies Ltd for materials received – and where it is owed money it is shown as a debit.

As it was the end of Colin's first year he and Sue wanted to know how well he had done. So, having proved that the books balanced, Sue's next job was to draw up the 'profit and loss statement'. The balance of the profit and loss statement will be the profit or loss they have made for the year.

Before she could do this, Colin had to value the stock of materials that he still had using the prices that they had cost him. Also, they had to decide how much to reduce the value of the van and the tools, as they had had a year's use out of them – this is called 'depreciation'. Before arriving at the figures for depreciation Colin had to speak to his accountant to find out how much the Inland Revenue would allow him to charge. This was because the amount of depreciation is charged against the profits of the business as an expense like electricity, petrol etc. The Revenue, quite rightly, need to ensure that depreciation is not being used purely as a means of reducing the amount of tax payable, so they have certain limits regarding the tax implications. This does not mean that a business cannot reduce the value of its property and equipment by however much it wants to, only that it will be restricted in the amount it can set off against its taxable profits.

From the profit and loss statement in exhibit 2.2 we can see that the gross profit for the year amounted to £18,700 and the net profit to £13,370, but this did not include Colin's labour, which was responsible for a large part of the income. This is because he was self-employed and the net profit of the business belonged to him. If he employed someone to help him with the plumbing work, then the wages of that person would have been shown in the first part of the statement next to the Purchases as part of the 'cost of sales' and would have reduced the gross profit by that amount. We shall see how Colin's drawings were dealt with when we look at his balance sheet.

In the second part of the profit and loss statement we can see that Colin paid Sue £1,500 for doing the paperwork, and was able to

Exhibit 2.2 Profit and loss statement as at 31 March 199X

Purchases	£22,000	Sales	£40,000
Less closing stock	700		
	21,300		
Gross profit	18,700		
	40,000		40,000
Motor running expenses	1,700	Gross profit	18,700
Office Wages	1,500		
Office Expenses	200		
Use of Accommodation	230		
Depreciation			
Van	1,500		
Tools and equipt	200		
Net profit for year	13,370		
	18,700		18,700

charge £230 for the use of his home as a workplace (Use of Accommodation). The amounts for the Use of Accommodation and Depreciation were not paid out of the business via the cheque book, they simply wore away as the equipment and furniture were used.

We are now in a position to look at the up-to-date financial position of Colin Wells' business at the end of his first year. This we do by means of a balance sheet which is a 'snapshot' of the book values of the assets owned and the liabilities owed by a business at a particular point in time (exhibit 2.3). We have set the balance sheet out in what has become the more usual form: that is, with the fixed assets and working capital at the top and the capital at the bottom. These used to be laid out side by side so that the totals of £11,600 were on the same line, showing that it balanced – hence the name balance sheet. Nowadays we tend to print reports etc. on A4 paper longways, so it is more convenient to put the two halves one above the other.

From Colin's profit and loss statement and his balance sheet we can see that, allowing for the fact that it was his first year, it went quite well. He was obviously quite busy and was able to take out £12,000 by

Exhibit 2.3 Colin Wells' balance sheet at 31 March

Fixed Assets				
Van at cost		6,000		
less depreciation		1,500	4,500	
Tools and equipment at cost		800		
less depreciation		200	600	5,100
Investments				
Building society account				3,000
Working Capital				
Current Assets				
Stock of materials		700		
Debtors		2,200		
Bank		1,100		
Cash		200	4,200	
Less current liabilities				
Creditors			700	3,500
				11,600
Financed by:				
Capital				
Balance as at 1 April 199X			10,000	
Add: Net profit for the year		13,370		
Less drawings	12,000			
Less use of accommodation	230	11,770	1,600	
Balance as at 31 March 199X + 1				11,600

way of drawings, and paid Sue £1,500 for doing the books (we saw this in the profit and loss statement).

We are not going to complicate the figures by concerning ourselves with income tax, V.A.T. and National Insurance at this stage.

Before we leave the subject of balance sheets we need to look at one for a limited company and note the differences from the one for the sole trader (see exhibit 2.4).

As we can see, the format is still basically the same. We have all of the items that make up the fixed assets, and to the total we add the figure for the working capital, which is made up of the current assets less the current liabilities.

Exhibit 2.4 MWC Limited, balance sheet as at 31 March 199X

Fixed Assets			
Land and buildings	235,000		
Plant and machinery	142,500		
Vehicles	62,000		
Computers	10,600		
Furniture and fittings	23,650	473,750	
Investments			
Shares in subsidiary		125,000	598,750
Working Capital			
Current assets			
Stocks	342,600		
Debtors	123,400		
Short-term investments	50,000		
Cash at bank and in hand	106,700	622,700	
Less current liabilities			
Trade creditors	113,700		
Loan interest	30,000		
Corporation Tax	46,600	190,300	432,400
			1,031,150
Financed by:			
Share capital			650,000
Reserves			181,150
Total shareholders' funds			831,150
Loan capital			200,000
			1,031,150

In the balance sheet for MWC Ltd we can see that the investment in the shares of a related company has been entered under the fixed assets; whereas the short-term investment, which relates to putting some spare money into an account where it can earn some interest, has been listed under the current assets. In the case of Colin Wells the building society investment was shown separately. This is because a sole trader is not legally obliged to set his or her accounts out in a certain order, while a limited company is. Colin wanted the balance of his building society account to be separate as it was the part of his original capital that he had not yet had to use.

In the balance sheet of MWC Ltd we can see what appears to be a very high figure for stocks. Whether this is in fact high or not will depend on the type of business that MWC Ltd are in. If they are manufacturers this figure could be broken down into raw materials and consumables, work in progress and finished goods. If they are wholesalers or retailers you would expect them to have money tied up in stock, but what if they have too much? When we look at ratios in chapter 5 we will examine ways of comparing stock levels against the sales turnover to check how efficiently the company is working.

SUMMARY

In this chapter we have seen that money becomes converted into stocks of materials, work in progress and debtors. Money is one of our most important resources and its use needs to be planned, monitored and controlled. Whilst this role is normally that of the finance department, all supervisors/first line managers have a responsibility for some of the resources into which the money is converted.

Organizational objectives ultimately are expressed in financial terms, but may be translated into more numeric terms for different departments, such as production targets. So supervisors/first line managers who have numeric objectives to achieve or to provide information on, will need also to consider the financial implications.

Supervisory Management Standards:

Unit 2 Contribute to the planning, monitoring and control of resources

Element 2.2 Monitor and control the use of resources

Unit 7 Provide information and advice for action towards meeting organizational objectives
Element 7.1 Obtain, evaluate, record and store information

In this chapter we have looked at:

- double entry bookkeeping
- the concept of the trial balance
- capital, share capital and loan capital
- fixed assets and current assets
- current liabilities
- working capital
- investments
- retained profits and reserves
- profit and loss statements, which showed us what had happened to the business over a specific accounting period
- the balance sheet, which is a summary of the book values of the assets owned and the liabilities owed by a business at a certain date

FURTHER READING

J. R. Dyson, *Accounting for Non-Accounting Students*, 2nd edn. Pitman, 1991.
Claude Hitching and Derek Stone, *Understanding Accounting*. Pitman, 1984.
Graham Mott, *Accounting for Non-Accountants*, 3rd edn. Kogan Page, 1990.

Chapter 3

Planning and Controlling the Money

Supervisory Management Standards	
Unit 2	Contribute to the planning, monitoring and control of resources
Element 2.1	Plan the use of resources
Element 2.2	Monitor and control the use of resources
Unit 7	Provide information and advice for action towards meeting organizational objectives
Element 7.1	Obtain, evaluate, record and store information
Element 7.2	Provide information and advice

So far we have looked at the profit and loss statement and the balance sheet. The profit and loss statement told us what had happened in the past in an accounting period to a certain date, and the balance sheet gave us a summary of the book values of the business at the close of business on a specified day. Both of these documents are part of the **financial accounting** process of the company. Financial accounting can be defined as the analysis, classification and recording of financial transactions of a business, and as such is concerned with the external transactions, like dealings with customers, suppliers and shareholders. The preparation of the profit and loss statement and the balance sheet are things we have to do for reasons we have already discussed. What they do not do is help us to plan and manage the business in the future; they only provide a starting point. This is where we move from financial accounting to **management account-**

ing. Management accounting is far more about preparing and presenting financial information in such a way as to assist the management of a business in formulating strategies, to help planning and controlling of the business, and to improve decision making. That all sounds very heavy and probably does not mean too much to you, so let's have a look at management accounting in action.

In the *In Charge* volume *Managing People* we discussed the fact that two of the main managerial functions are planning and controlling. The key managerial planning tool which is then used to monitor and control the business is the budget.

BUDGETS

A budget is a plan in financial and numerical terms which forecasts the results of a specified future trading period. Usually a number of budgets will be prepared covering different areas of the business: for example, there will be separate budgets for sales, production costs and administration. A sales budget forecasts the anticipated sales for each week or month throughout the period of the budget. From this the level of production and the production costs can be forecast and the overall production budget drawn up. These budgets may be further divided into sales of each product, amounts and costs of materials, production labour, packaging costs, distribution costs etc. These are then coordinated into one master budget which represents the company's plan for that period of trading. The directors and/or senior management have to evaluate the master budget to make sure that it is realistic, and have to pay particular attention to the limiting factor(s).

A **limiting factor** is the item that restricts how much we can produce and sell in goods and services. If we cannot sell all the goods that we are capable of producing, our limiting factor would be the total of anticipated sales. But if we can sell everything we can produce but cannot get enough raw materials, then our limiting factor would be the amount of raw materials. In a travel tour company, sales might be limited by the number of plane seats we are allocated to particular destinations, so the limiting factor would be the number of plane seats.

The budget for each department needs to be drawn up by making use of the knowledge and experience of the supervisors/first line managers and managers who are in that department. This will include looking at the actual figures for the previous period and revising them for the new period in the light of known and likely changes in the level of activity and costs. Obviously information will need to be given in advance as to what the limiting factor is and what level of growth is expected.

When all of the budgets have been completed the coordination process must then take place. It will be found that the budgets do not fit together to form a cohesive plan without adjustments to some or all of them. Negotiations and discussions should then take place to alter each budget until each department is in agreement. This agreement is very important, because the supervisors/first line managers and managers who are responsible for controlling the budget in each department – these people are known as 'budget holders' – must be committed to the figures if they are going to make them work. If a budget is imposed on a department it is very often disregarded by them, and the system of budgetary control breaks down.

Once the budgets have been agreed they then become the tools by which progress is monitored in that period. Most companies and organizations enter their budgets onto a computer programme which

Budget Report for the month of ________							
	Current month's figures			Cumulative figures			
Item	Budget	Actual	Variance + or −	Budget	Actual	Variance + or −	Explanation

Figure 3.1 Budget variation report

provides them with regular printouts of the actual figures compared with the budget ones. Explanations of them are then sought for any significant variances. Cumulative figures are also maintained so that trends can be identified and corrective action taken where necessary (see figure 3.1).

Obviously the figures are never going to be exactly as they forecast, and small variances are quite acceptable. However, the need to alert directors and senior management to significant differences can be vital to the survival of the business and the sooner the situation is recognized the more time, and usually the more options, are available for correcting it.

THINK POINT

If you were asked to draw up a list of all the payments you and your partner make during the course of a year relating to your home life, which ones would you know and which ones would you have to consult your partner over? Which months are they due and what records would you have to consult to find any missing ones? The list below may help you with this task.

Housekeeping
Mortgage payments
Rent
Council Tax
Water rates
House insurance
Gas
Electricity
Telephone
Pocket money
Coal
Car repayments
Car tax
Car insurance
Car service
Decorating and repairs
Personal loan repayments
Hire purchase payments
Clothing
Holidays
Birthdays
Christmas
Life insurance
Health insurance
Bank interest and charges
Television licence
Club subscriptions
Motoring associations
Newspapers and magazines
Petrol
Savings

As we can see, very few people would be able to complete such a list on their own or without good records to refer to. The Think Point should have brought it home to us just how necessary it is for whoever is responsible for the budgets, to make enquiries of his or her colleagues, to ensure that nothing is overlooked.

Few of us have so much surplus income that we can just spend whatever we like, and it is therefore necessary to plan ahead. The same applies to companies, which have the additional disadvantage of usually having to wait for the money from their sales to be paid to them whilst still having to pay wages, salaries etc.

CASH AVAILABILITY OR LIQUIDITY

Many businesses fail as a result of not realizing, far enough ahead, the amount of cash they need to have available. They continue to take on and carry out profitable work and contracts without concerning themselves with the very basic question of cash availability, or 'liquidity'. The first time they become aware of a liquidity problem may be when they receive a letter from their bank manager about the size of their overdraft or, even worse, telling them that the bank has been unable to pay their cheques for lack of funds. Sometimes it can be a demand for tax due on the previous year's profits that causes the crisis; or the three-monthly V.A.T. return that needs paying but for which no provision has been made, although they should have expected it. At that time they might be extremely busy with work and have huge amounts invested in stock, work in progress and debtors. But you cannot pay your bills or your wages with stock.

When we looked at working capital in the balance sheets of Colin Wells and MWC Ltd we saw money tied up in stocks of materials, money owed by customers and money owed to creditors. Also included were the balances of money in the bank, the cash we had available in the business and the money invested on a short-term basis to gain interest. The measure of liquidity is how easily an asset can be turned into cash, so these last three items are the most important in this respect. Equally important would be the amount of any unused overdraft facility at the bank, as cash could be drawn against it.

Debtors are turned into cash when they pay their bills. In normal trading conditions this should not be a problem, because a pattern of payment will have been established. Depending on what trade or type of business you are in, you will know approximately how many days credit is usual before you have to start chasing the customer for payment. However, when times are hard (for example, during a recession), debtors take longer and longer to pay and, worse, many become bad debts. If the length of time for debtors to pay during normal trading times is, say, 30 days, and during a recession this becomes 80–90 days, it is easy to see what effect this would have on the working capital. If we apply this to the balance sheet of Colin Wells, which we have repeated in exhibit 3.1, we can see that the

Exhibit 3.1 Colin Wells' balance sheet at 31 March 199X

Fixed Assets				
Van at cost		6,000		
less depreciation		1,500	4,500	
Tools and equipment at cost		800		
less depreciation		200	600	5,100
Investments				
Building society account				3,000
Working Capital				
Current assets				
Stock of materials		700		
Debtors		2,200		
Bank		1,100		
Cash		200	4,200	
Less current liabilities				
Creditors			700	3,500
				11,600
Financed by:				
Capital				
Balance as at 1 April 199?			10,000	
Add: Net profit for the year		13,370		
Less drawings	12,000			
Less use of accommodation	230	11,770	1,600	
Balance as at 31 March 199X				11,600

figure for debtors would approximately triple from £2,200 to around £6,600 which would wipe out his cash, bank balance and building society account investment. Fortunately, Colin's business has just about enough cash and balances to be able to withstand it, but many other businesses would have failed in these circumstances.

CREDIT CONTROL

Whilst we are considering the subject of debtors it is worthwhile recalling that a customer only becomes a debtor after he or she has been invoiced for the work. All too often businesses are very slow with their paper work, and do not send out invoices until weeks or even months after the work has been carried out. This negligence tends to cause the customer to regard the bill as non-urgent, and it therefore takes even longer to collect the money.

The first reaction of many businesses to a situation where they are having to give longer credit to their customers, is to take more time to pay their bills. In larger companies and organizations this is far more possible than in businesses the size of Colin's. Few would want to upset a potentially large customer by chasing for their money too hard, or even taking legal action to recover the debt. In Colin's case, the increase in his debtors total may have arisen because some of his large customers are not paying their bills. It would be difficult for Colin to run up much higher totals for his creditors, as his suppliers could easily refuse to supply him with goods on credit unless previous invoices were paid. Also, if a business took legal action against him to recover a debt, it could cause him to be black-listed and prevent him from receiving any credit in the future.

CASH SHORTAGES OR LIQUIDITY CRISES

In the past when businesses have experienced cash shortages they have run down their stocks of raw materials and finished goods, but this is less possible today. The introduction of 'just in time' and similar systems – which are discussed in *In Charge, Managing Operations* – have resulted in massive destocking over the last few years and have therefore largely removed this option.

The fixed assets are the least liquid assets. Where businesses own surplus premises they could try to sell them to raise cash for additional working capital, but this takes time to arrange. Furthermore, if the need for the cash has arisen as a result of a recession, then the chances are that the premises will be difficult to sell and will not realize a very good price.

It is in these circumstances that many businesses would need to make arrangements with their banks for overdraft facilities or increased overdraft facilities. These may take time to arrange. In the first place it is probable that an appointment will have to be made and, secondly, in the case of a small- or medium-sized business, the bank may want security for the overdraft facility, such as a second mortgage on the owner's house(s), which could take weeks or even months to complete. Most larger businesses will already have facilities with their bankers, and increases may be easier to arrange, but even here there can be delays. The size of facility they require could mean that agreement to it must be taken at the head office level or local head office level of the bank, and security, such as a legal charge over land and buildings, might be considered necessary.

Obviously the greater the warning a business has that it is going to need cash, the greater the number of options it is likely to have for obtaining it. This is one of the places where management accounting can help.

THE CASH FLOW PROCESS

The cash flow forecast, or 'cash budget' is an essential planning tool for all businesses, whether they are large or small, rich or poor. In this chapter we have so far discussed the need to allow as much time as possible to enable us to make arrangements for additional cash when necessary. We have not looked at the possible implications if we have *too much* cash at any one time.

Many of the largest companies in the world have treasurer's departments whose main function is to identify cash surpluses. They then invest the money at the best possible rates of return, according to how long it is going to be available. Often they convert it into other currencies according to the movements in exchange rates. Where it is a group of companies, the surplus may be sent by one company in the group to another, therefore removing the need to pay interest to a bank or other lender. Some companies even make more profit by investing their surplus cash than they do from carrying out their normal business.

To be able to identify the surpluses and shortages it is necessary to forecast the amounts of cash that will come into the business or organization, the amounts of cash that will go out, and when those movements will take place. Except in small businesses like Colin Wells', no one person will have all the answers. The accountant, manager, partner or whoever has this responsibility, must make enquiries of the budget holders in the same way as when constructing other budgets.

Case Note 4

In chapter 1 mention was made of how Colin, Sue, Jack and Karen Wells started a limited company called Wells (Plumbers) Ltd. Colin and Jack were able to put into the company the vans, equipment, tools and stock from their partnership business, and they decided to add their personal cars, both of which were of the estate type, to provide additional vehicles the company required. The value of the vehicles, equipment, tools and stock, were topped up with their savings, so that between them they had £20,000 to put into the company as share capital.

Instead of taking on additional help at the beginning, it was decided that Karen, who had recently completed her training as a plumber and central heating engineer, should work full-time for the company. The balance sheet shown in exhibit 3.2 is at the end of the first year of trading by the limited company.

During the year the company had rented a lock-up garage with storage and office accommodation. This involved it in the expense of buying furniture and fittings, but it had been able to buy these quite cheaply at an auction sale of second-hand office furniture. Apart from their share capital we can see that Colin and Jack loaned the company £6,000 each. This was done with the idea that as the profits accumulated they would be able to withdraw this money. The capital position has been added to by the retention of £7,700 of profits which are entered under 'Reserves'.

The balance sheet was prepared by Sue Wells and will need to be amended after she obtains advice from their accountants on company taxation and allowances. Sue found an accounting software package for the computer, which enabled her to produce the balance sheet from the accounts, immediately after the year end.

The four directors set aside the whole of one weekend at the

Exhibit 3.2 Wells (Plumbers) Ltd balance sheet as at 31 March 199X

Fixed Assets at cost			
Vehicles		30,500	
Equipment and tools		3,500	
Furniture and fittings		1,250	
Computer		1,050	
Total cost			36,300
Less depreciation to date			6,100
Current written down value			30,200
Working Capital			
Current assets			
Stock		2,800	
Debtors		9,000	
Cash in hand and at bank		1,500	
Total current assets			13,300
Less current liabilities			
Trade creditors		3,800	
Total current liabilities			3,800
Net working capital			9,500
			39,700
Financed by:			
Share Capital			20,000
Reserves (retained profit)			7,700
Total shareholders' funds			27,700
Loan capital			
C. Wells	6,000		
J. Wells	6,000		12,000
Capital employed			39,700

beginning of April to get together to plan the next year. Their biggest concern was whether they would have enough cash to do the things they wanted to, so they knew that they needed to prepare a cash flow forecast. However, they recognized that first they needed to agree on their goals for the next year so that they were all striving for the same things.

They decided to start off by brainstorming all of the things they would like to achieve over the next year. They then went through the list and agreed which of these would be their goals and then put them in order of priority. The goals included the expansion of the domestic work and the maintenance work for shops, letting agencies etc. Having done this, they worked out some figures as to what the costs would be and started to do some calculations involving the balance of the bank account.

It was at this point that they realized that they could not prepare a *cash flow forecast* until they had prepared all of the other budgets. They needed a *sales budget*, broken down month by month, to be able to work out the money coming into the company and the money going out for materials; they needed a budget for the motor vehicles, and another for the office expenses and overheads (such as rent and electricity). They then realized that they would need another for their salaries and the payment of income tax and national insurance, and yet another for additional tools, equipment and the cost of changing one of the vehicles.

Even the sales budget needed to be divided between domestic jobs and commercial ones. They had learned early on that they needed to collect the cash or cheque for domestic jobs whilst they were on-site at the customer's and, in the case of new central heating installations and bathroom suites, they needed the materials paid for in advance of fitting them. Commercial jobs involve sending in an invoice, and they were getting to know who would pay them within 30 days and who would keep them waiting longer for their money. Commercial jobs were bigger and more profitable, but domestic jobs paid straightaway and so did not tie up working capital in the form of debtors.

They decided that if they jointly agreed the sales targets for the year and broke the figures down onto a monthly basis, then each of them could be responsible for drawing up the budgets for the different areas of work. As Sue was In Charge of all of the office work and salaries she knew more about what the costs and requirements were likely to be in that area than the others, so she would draw up the *office expenses budget* and the *salaries budget*. Similarly, Karen was In

Charge of the domestic plumbing work: whilst both Colin and Jack had more experience than she did and helped with some of the work at peak times, it was recognized as being her area of responsibility, so she would draw up a *materials budget* and *motor expenses budget* for the domestic work. Colin and Jack would divide the commercial work between them. Colin would concentrate on the new installation work for small building contractors whereas Jack was In Charge of developing the maintenance work for shops, offices and letting agencies etc. Both Colin and Jack would draw up a *materials budget* and *motor expenses budget* for their areas, based on the sales figures that they were all going to agree first of all.

It was decided that when all four of them had completed their provisional budgets, each would then present them to the others and explain the thinking behind their estimates. The four of them would then discuss the figures and adjustments could be made where necessary.

Jack commented that this procedure made it sound as if they were senior departmental managers in a big corporation, but the others pointed out to him that they all expected the company to grow, and that it was better to get used to doing things properly from the beginning.

THE SALES BUDGET

In drawing up the sales budget they decided that the factor that was likely to limit them the most was not the availability of work, as they had been turning work down, but the amount of work that Colin, Jack and Karen could physically carry out. They discussed taking on an additional plumber, but decided against this as they were not sure that the additional amount of work available would justify it. Instead they agreed to start a school leaver on to assist Karen in September if the level of work continued to warrant it, but in the meantime Colin and Jack would help out as required. They liked the idea of training their own people, or 'growing their own timber', as Colin put it, rather than having to convert someone, already trained, to their ways of working and their standards. However, they decided that whilst this was a preferred option, they would not include it in their main budgets at this time but would do some additional calculations in case they did implement it.

They based the sales budget on past experience and expected

growth but tried to err on the cautious side. The first few months of the sales budget after they agreed it looked like that shown in exhibit 3.3.

They had allowed for holidays in July and August – both their own and holiday close-downs by building contractors.

Exhibit 3.3 Sales budget (all figures in £000s)

Month	April	May	June	July	August	Sept
Domestic	6.0	5.0	5.0	4.0	2.5	5.0
Commercial						
New devs.	5.0	5.0	5.0	3.5	3.0	5.0
Maintenance	2.0	2.5	2.5	3.0	2.0	3.0
Total	13.0	12.5	12.5	10.5	7.5	13.0

CASH FLOW FORECAST

As agreed, they then separated to draw up the other budgets for materials, motor expenses etc. based on the level of activity agreed in the sales budget. After they had presented their proposals to the others and made any amendments, they next brought all of the figures together to produce the cash budget or cash flow forecast (exhibit 3.4).

We can see from the cash flow forecast that the company's bank account should be in credit throughout the year, and that there are periods when it would be prudent for them to transfer some surplus money into an interest-yielding account.

Providing all goes reasonably to plan it should be possible for them to take on the school leaver and, although it will take time for him or her to fully earn their pay, the company can afford to treat this as an investment for the future.

After they had completed all of the budgets Sue worked out a forecast profit and loss statement which showed a satisfactory profit figure. This they were satisfied with, bearing in mind that they could either increase their salaries if they looked like paying too much corporation tax or alter the timing of their additional salary payments if the company needed more working capital.

Exhibit 3.4 Cash flow forecast, April to September (£000s)

Month	April	May	June	July	Aug	Sept
Balance at start of month	1.5[a]	4.1	6.5	1.35	3.95	5.05
Plus Receipts						
Domestic work	6.0	5.0	5.0	4.0	2.5	5.0
Commercial work	6.0[b]	6.5	7.25	7.5	7.0	5.75
Total	12.0	11.5	12.25	11.5	9.5	10.75
Less Payments						
Materials	3.8[c]	3.5	3.4	3.4	3.0	2.0
Salaries and Nat. Ins.	4.0	4.0	4.0	4.0	4.0	4.0
Vehicle expenses	0.6	0.6	0.6	0.5	0.4	0.6
Office cost incl. rent	1.0	1.0	1.0	1.0	1.0	1.0
Capital expenditure			5.0[d]			
VAT payments			3.4			2.7
Total	9.4	9.1	17.4	8.9	8.4	10.3
Balance at end of month	4.1[e]	6.5	1.35	3.95	5.05	5.50

Notes

[a] This balance has been taken from the balance sheet as being the balance of cash in hand on 31st March.

[b] We were told earlier that the domestic work is paid for by the customer at the time whereas some of the commercial work is paid one month later, some two months later. This means that the receipts for the commercial work for April include some work that was carried out and invoiced in February, and some in March.

[c] Trade creditors are paid in this case after 30 days, so this figure has been taken from the balance sheet.

[d] The four directors have decided to change one of the four vehicles each year and have therefore allowed £5,000 for this.

[e] The balance at the start of the month plus the receipts and less the expenditure gives us the balance at the end of the month, which is then carried forward to the start of the next month.

Cash flow forecast, October to March (£000s)

Month	Oct	Nov	Dec	Jan	Feb	Mar	Totals
Balance							
1st month	5.5	3.55	6.55	6.7	11.1	13.85	
Plus Receipts							
Domestic work	5.0	5.0	5.0	5.5	5.5	5.5	59.00
Commercial work	6.5	8.5	9.0	9.0	8.75	8.5	90.25
Total	11.5	13.5	14.0	14.5	14.25	14.0	149.25
Less Payments							
Materials	3.8	4.8	4.7	4.4	4.8	5.1	46.70
Salaries	8.0[f]	4.0	4.0	4.0	4.0	8.0[f]	56.00
Vehicle expenses	0.65	0.7	0.7	0.7	0.7	0.7	7.45
Office incl. rent	1.0	1.0	1.0	1.0	1.0	1.0	12.00
Capital expend.					1.0	4.0[g]	10.00
VAT payments			3.45			3.35	12.90
Total	13.45	10.5	13.85	10.1	10.5	22.15	145.05
Balance end month	3.55	6.55	6.7	11.1	13.85	5.7	

(The balance at the start of the month + total receipts − total payments = balance at the end of the month.)

[f] In these two cases the four directors propose to pay themselves extra money to reduce the amount of profit on which the company would have to pay corporation tax.

[g] This item of £4,000 is where Colin and Jack are proposing to withdraw part of their loans to the company. This way they can get their money out of the company without paying tax, but only to the extent of the loans they have made.

Sue took charge of entering all the budgets onto the computer, so that each month they would be able to print out how the actual figures compared with budgeted figures and take any necessary corrective action.

> **THINK POINT**
>
> If the company found out in April that one of the building companies for whom they did work had gone into liquidation owing them £3,000, what effect would this have on their balance of cash at the end of June, and what steps could they take to minimize the effects?

(They could defer the capital expenditure on a new vehicle for a while or obtain an overdraft from their bankers.)

Budgets and the cash flow forecast are examples of where management accounting takes over from financial accounting to provide information for running the business. In the following chapters we will see other examples of this.

SUMMARY

We have seen in previous chapters that many of the resources for which we are responsible can be converted into cash by the business cycle – stock when sold becomes debtors, debtors when they pay become cash or money in the bank. In this chapter we have looked at how we can plan, monitor and control the use of resources through budgets and the cash flow forecast. Our knowledge and experience should be important in providing senior management with a clear picture of the budgetary needs of our team or department, but we must remember that there is rarely enough money to meet all needs and compromises must be made.

Supervisory Management Standards:

Unit 2 Contribute to the planning, monitoring and control of resources

Element 2.1 Plan the use of resources
Element 2.2 Monitor and control the use of resources

Unit 7 Provide information and advice for action towards meeting organizational objectives
Element 7.1 Obtain, evaluate, record and store information
Element 7.2 Provide information and advice

In this chapter we have looked at:

- the difference between the financial accounting function and the management accounting function
- the budgeting process
- monitoring the business by use of budgets
- business liquidity
- the cash flow forecast

FURTHER READING

John Arnold and Tony Hope, *Accounting for Management Decisions*, 2nd edn. Prentice Hall, 1990.

J. R. Dyson, *Accounting for Non-Accounting Students*, 2nd edn. Pitman, 1991.

Alan Pizzey, *Cost and Management Accounting*, 3rd edn. P.C.P., 1990.

Chapter 4
Costs and Costing

Supervisory Management Standards	
Unit 2	Contribute to the planning, monitoring and control of resources
Element 2.1	Plan the use of resources
Element 2.2	Monitor and control the use of resources
Unit 7	Provide information and advice for action towards meeting organizational objectives
Element 7.1	Obtain, evaluate, record and store information
Element 7.2	Provide information and advice

The marketplace for nearly all goods and services has moved away from the days when manufacturers and suppliers could sell more or less everything they chose to make or provide, towards a situation where the customer can dictate what they are prepared to buy. This trend has brought about a change in the way in which businesses operate. No longer can manufacturers have very long production runs, as their goods are required in a range of colours and specifications, and they must respond rapidly to the changing demands of the market and to innovation from increased competition. The advent of 'just in time', which is covered in *In Charge, Managing Operations*, has also resulted in manufacturers having to produce their products in small batches, which in turn means resetting machines quickly to minimize the loss of production. In this situation the dangers of not pricing products correctly can easily result in either selling at a loss or failing to sell through overpricing.

In this chapter we are going to apply some common-sense rules and procedures to the subject of costs. Our case study for this will be a company called Topicflex Ltd, who manufacture various types of packaging materials, including plastic wrap, plastic inserts, cartons and boxes. However, the concepts and the procedures we are going to use apply to all types of businesses and organizations.

COST UNITS

A cost unit is the unit of manufacture, service or time to which costs can be allocated and for which it is convenient to express a cost per unit. That all sounds a bit like a dictionary quote, so let's have a look at some examples. When asked to quote for a contract, Topicflex needs to have some definite volumes that are relevant to the type of business. For example, to make and supply plastic wrap packaging to china manufacturers they might quote them a price of so much per 100 metre roll of a certain width. In this case they would calculate their costs of production for making one roll, or, if they had a lot of customers for this product, they might base their costs on making ten rolls. Either the one roll or the ten rolls, whichever they chose, would be their *cost unit*. Moulded plastic inserts to go in the cartons to protect perfume bottles might be quoted and costed per thousand or ten thousand, whichever is more appropriate.

Similarly, a bricklayer might use a cost unit of so much per thousand bricks, or for repointing a wall (i.e. cutting out the top layer of the old mortar and replacing it with new) his cost unit might be a square metre of wall repointed. He would therefore calculate the size of the brickwork to be repointed and quote to repoint x number of square metres at £—.

COST CENTRES

A cost centre is a clearly-defined part of a business or organization which is under the charge of one person and to which it is convenient to allocate certain costs. At the Head Office level of a large company each factory or group of branches might be a cost centre. Each of these will then be broken down at the local level into smaller cost centres. Sometimes this will be done on a departmental basis, but this is not necessarily the case. Different cost centres may be responsible for different parts of the production process: stores may be a separate cost centre, so may the despatch unit, the canteen, the maintenance unit, personnel department, accounts, administration, security etc.

One person can be a cost centre – for example, the managing director will have the costs of his salary, national insurance, pension, expenses, office, secretary, secretary's office, telephones, car, petrol etc. One production line or even one machine could be a cost centre – for example, one of the very large printing machines.

The importance of having each cost centre under the control of one person is that targets can be set and budgets agreed, and it is up to that individual to manage it successfully or be held accountable. This may sound very authoritarian, but costs are like the rabbits in Australia – let them loose and they multiply very rapidly, and before you know it they have totally undermined a profitable business.

Whilst it is recommended that one person is responsible for each cost centre, the control and reduction of costs should be the concern of everyone, just like the maintenance and improvement of customer care and quality. Finding ways of controlling and reducing costs should be one of the key areas for the quality circles and product improvement groups. (Customer care, quality, quality circles and problem solving groups are all covered in *In Charge, Managing Operations*.)

All of the relevant costs will be charged to the cost centre. Each shop in a chain of shops will be charged out for the wages, national insurance, pension contributions, maternity pay and so forth of the staff, the stock supplied to it (including a share of the transport, the rent, cost of maintenance and insurance), plus a portion of the head office costs which relate to them. For example, the costs of the personnel department may be charged out to the branches at so much per member of staff they employ.

If a cost centre is part of a larger unit (for example, the word processing and photocopying unit within a head office), it will have various costs allocated to it. These will be on a variety of bases, in addition to all of the obvious costs, like wages, salaries and stationery. It will be charged with a portion of the rent, probably according to how many square feet, square yards or square metres it occupies – so asking for more space might not be such a good idea, even though it would be nice to have a larger office. The portion of the lighting, heating and electricity might be on the same basis, while the electricity might be allocated according to the number of machines the department has. Other costs may be charged on a head count basis. Sometimes the allocation of costs is done on the basis of what is easiest for the management or cost accountant, and does not truly reflect the usage made by that cost centre.

THINK POINT

Which cost centre are you employed in and how are costs apportioned to it?

COST ELEMENTS

Costs can be divided up into three distinct and separate elements – materials costs, labour costs and expenses.

1 Materials costs are for those materials that are used up in the course of the work and do not include the depreciation of fixed assets.
2 Labour costs usually include the wages and salaries, but some companies and organizations might exclude the manager's salary from a particular cost centre and see it as part of the head office costs instead.
3 Expenses costs cover all of the remaining costs.

The three cost elements are then subdivided into direct and indirect costs. So we then have

- direct materials and indirect materials
- direct labour and indirect labour
- direct expenses and indirect expenses

The three direct cost elements relate solely to the process of making the product or providing the service.

The three elements of indirect costs – indirect materials, indirect labour and indirect expenses are referred to as **overheads**.

To understand how these fit in, let us look at some examples.

In Topicflex Ltd when they are making the plastic inserts to go in the perfume boxes the *direct materials* would be the plastic they use for it, whereas the machine lubricants and any consumable tools and stationery would be classed as *indirect materials*. The *direct labour* costs would include the wages for the people working the machines, whereas the supervisor would be classed as *indirect labour*. If in this case the supervisor actually worked a machine as well, then strictly speaking it would be necessary to divide the costs between direct and indirect. The power used by the machines making the items would be *direct expenses*, whereas the heating and lighting, factory rent etc. would be regarded as *indirect expenses*.

In a supermarket the goods sold would obviously be classed as *direct materials* but the machine tally-rolls and carrier bags would be an *indirect materials* cost. The check-out staff would be the *direct labour* and the store management and shelf fillers etc. would be the *indirect labour* costs. In this example all of the expenses, such as cleaning and electricity, would probably be indirect ones.

In Wells (Plumbers) Ltd, if Karen was costing out the installation of a central heating system, the boiler, radiators, piping and joints would all be *direct material* costs, and the PTFE tape, saw blades etc. would be *indirect material* costs, as they would be used on a number of different jobs. The labour used in actually fitting the system would be *direct labour*, but the time taken to visit the customer to measure up, do the paperwork and quote for the work would be classed as *indirect labour*. *Direct expenses* could include the cost of hiring a disc grinder to cut the old system out, whereas *indirect expenses* could include the vehicle costs etc.

We can see from these examples that *direct costs* are those that can be easily identified as being essential parts of particular products and services, while the *indirect costs* need to be shared out amongst a number of products.

It is important that each product and service is accurately costed to ensure that we get the pricing right. To be underpriced could mean that we are producing at a loss so that the more goods we produce the more money we lose. Alternatively, if we are overpriced we are in danger of not selling the goods we produce or attracting competition in.

The largest companies have cost accountants whose job it is to collect up and allocate the costs, to enable an accurate picture of the product or service costs to be established, and to check the cost performance of each cost centre. In large- to medium-sized companies this work will be carried out by the management or financial accountants, or even by directors or managers, if at all.

MARGINAL COSTING

Marginal costing is not a method of calculating costs but more a means of presenting cost information in a certain way. It makes use of costs that are divided into two categories – *fixed costs* and *variable costs* – and relates them to the volumes of output.

Fixed and variable costs

Fixed costs tend not to vary much with the level of turnover within certain ranges. They relate to the things you have to pay even if production has stopped or has not yet started.

For example, if a company opens a new shop and takes on the staff, it will be committed to paying the rent and basic wages, even though it has yet to sell anything. It will also have all of the overhead costs relating to the head office. These costs are termed 'fixed' costs because they will not vary as a direct result of the amount of business activity until such a time as trade is so busy that they need to employ more staff or expand the shop.

Many overhead costs will vary as a result of factors other than the level of business activity in the shop. For example, the Head Office might change its stationery and therefore its stationery costs will vary, but as the change is not a result of the level of business activity it is classed as fixed costs and not variable costs.

It does not affect the administration costs, personnel department costs or the finance department costs if Topicflex Ltd make 100 rolls of plastic wrap in a day or 200 rolls, because they are 'fixed' costs.

Variable costs are those which vary in direct proportion to the level of activity in production or sales. If a shop doubles the number of items it sells, then the costs relating to its purchases must go up accordingly, as must its delivery costs etc.

If a coach company decides to run a day trip to Blackpool to see the lights, its variable costs will be those that it has taken on purely as a result of that decision. These might or might not include the wages for the driver, depending on whether he or she was being paid anyway and might otherwise have been sitting around. They would include overtime for the driver if this was required, plus any refreshments for the driver. Also included in the variable costs would be the fuel and oil used for the trip, plus any parking costs and extra cleaning of the coach. Any special advertising of the trip and commission to ticket agents would also be included. The additional mileage would probably call for additional maintenance, so a portion of the next service would also relate to this trip. However, if the maintenance facility was owned by the company, only the cost of any materials used in the maintenance would be variable costs, as the other costs of the maintenance department would be regarded as a fixed cost that had to be paid anyway.

The most important learning point from the study of fixed and variable costs is that, because fixed costs do not vary as a result of the level of business activity within certain ranges of output, the more items that are produced and sold, the more items the fixed costs are spread between. This in turn increases the amount of profit that is made per item.

Suppose Topicflex Ltd made only wrap packaging, and during the first week in April it made 350 rolls, while during the second it made 450 rolls. If the variable costs amounted to, say, £20 per roll, and all of the fixed costs for the company averaged, say, £2,000 per week, the overall situation would look like that in exhibit 4.1.

Exhibit 4.1

	Week 1	Week 2
Number of rolls produced	350	450
	£	£
Fixed costs	2,000	2,000
Variable costs @ £20 per roll	7,000	9,000
Total costs	9,000	11,000

Total cost per roll:

$$\text{Week 1} = \frac{9{,}000}{350} = £25.71\text{p}$$

$$\text{Week 2} = \frac{11{,}000}{450} = £24.44\text{p}$$

In exhibit 4.1 we can see that, whilst the variable costs increased from £9,000 to £11,000 because of the additional 100 rolls produced, the fixed costs remained the same at £2,000. This meant that when we divided the total costs out, each roll during the second week cost £1.27 less to produce because we are spreading the fixed costs out over more units. As a result, if Topicflex were selling them at the same price as in week 1, they would be making an additional £1.27 profit per roll.

CONTRIBUTION

Following on from the division of costs into fixed and variable is the concept of 'contribution'. Contribution is the difference between sales income and variable cost. If we use the example of the rolls of wrap again, and if, say, Topicflex sold them at £30 per roll, the contribution per roll would be £10.

Selling price £30 minus Variable cost £20 = Contribution £10

This contribution is first of all made to paying the fixed costs, and after that it is a contribution to profit.

Let's have a look at the example of weeks 1 and 2 again (exhibit 4.2).

Exhibit 4.2

	Week 1	Week 2
Number of rolls produced	350	450
	£	£
Sales income @ £30	10,500	13,500
Less variable costs @ £20 per roll	7,000	9,000
Contribution	3,500	4,500
Fixed costs	2,000	2,000
Profit	1,500	2,500

In this example we can see that at £30 per roll the company was making satisfactory profits. We can also see that at the higher volume in week 2 it could more easily cut its price if it needed to. Because Topicflex has worked out its costings accurately, it could easily judge by how much it could reduce the selling price and still make a satisfactory profit.

Once we know what the fixed and variable costs are we can draw up a chart of the various sales/production volumes (exhibit 4.3).

We have used simple prices and quantities in this example, and we can very easily see from the trend that the point at which it would just cover all of its costs at this price would be sales of 200 rolls per week. This is called the 'break-even point'.

Exhibit 4.3

Number of rows @ £30	250	300	350	400	450	500
Sales income	7,500	9,000	10,500	12,000	13,500	15,000
Variable cost	5,000	6,000	7,000	8,000	9,000	10,000
Contribution	2,500	3,000	3,500	4,000	4,500	5,000
Fixed costs	2,000	2,000	2,000	2,000	2,000	2,000
Profit	500	1,000	1,500	2,000	2,500	3,000

BREAK-EVEN POINT

The break-even point is the point at which the sales income equals the total costs, both variable and fixed. If Topicflex dropped below this it would be running at a loss. We could also have plotted the figures on a break-even chart like the one in figure 4.1.

In the break-even chart the horizontal axis shows the number of rolls sold and the vertical axis shows the sales income. We start by

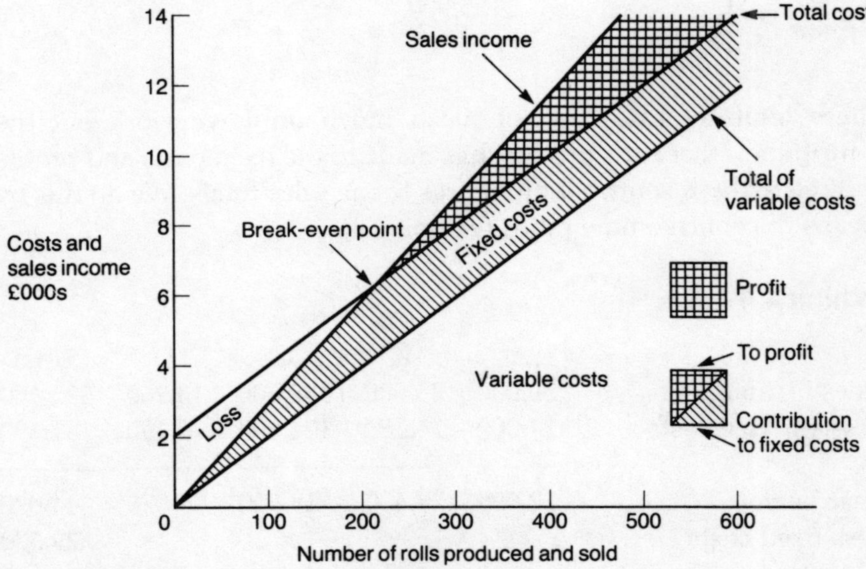

Figure 4.1 Marginal costing break-even chart

plotting the points for the variable costs at the various sales figures shown on the horizontal axis, and then join them up. Then parallel to this we put in the line for the fixed costs, which in this case are £2,000. As we have put the fixed costs on top of the variable costs this last line we have drawn represents the total costs (variable costs plus fixed costs). If we now plot the sales income figures on the chart we can see that the sales line crosses the total cost line at 200 rolls, and this is our break-even point.

If we apply the concept of contribution to a company that has, say, four products, we can see how decisions can more easily be made with the benefit of these figures.

For example, if Topicflex has four products A, B, C and D:

Product	A	B	C	D
Sales price per item	£3.00	2.4p	92p	£3.40
Variable cost per item	£2.00	1.8p	80p	2.10
Contribution per item	£1.00	0.6p	12p	1.30

During the first three months of its current year of trading it has produced and sold:

	Items
Product A	12,000
B	1,400,000
C	155,000
D	3,900

These totals of sales do not mean much until we work out the contribution that each product has made to the fixed costs and profits and relate these contribution figures to the sales totals. We do this by means of profit/volume ratios (exhibit 4.4).

Exhibit 4.4

	A	B	C	D	Total
Sales income	36,000	33,600	142,600	13,260	225,460
Less variable costs	24,000	25,200	124,000	8,190	181,390
Contribution	12,000	8,400	18,600	5,070	44,070
Less fixed costs					29,570
Profit					14,500

PROFIT/VOLUME RATIO

The profit/volume ratio is calculated by using the formula:

$$\frac{\text{Contribution}}{\text{Selling price}} \times \frac{100}{1}$$

If we ranked the four products in the order of highest percentage contribution to sales income, or the profit/volume ratio, using the Topicflex figures given above, the results would be:

Product D = 38.24%
A = 33.33%
B = 25%
C = 13.04%

We can now see that Product C, which has the smallest profit to volume ratio of 13.04%, produces 42% of the total *contribution* as a result of the larger turnover. In comparison, Product D, which has a high profit to volume ratio of 38.24%, only produces 11.5% of the total contribution. These product costs would give the management of Topicflex a good starting-point if they needed to find ways of increasing profits. Also, if they were up to full capacity in the factory, they might concentrate on producing more of the products with the highest percentage of contribution per item – providing, of course, that they could sell them.

One of the most important things about the use of 'marginal costing' and the concept of 'contribution' is that as soon as sufficient items have been sold for their contributions to cover the fixed costs, then all contributions thereafter are contributions to profit. This in turn means that companies having reached the break-even point could then take on work with a lower profit margin, if they had the capacity to do so, without the need to increase the fixed costs. For example, if Topicflex had reached its break-even point of 200 rolls of wrap per week on firm long-term contracts, and was asked to quote for a contract to produce 100 rolls per week for a customer, it would know that anything it charged over its variable cost figure of £20 per roll would be profit.

Marginal costing is particularly useful on those occasions when the company is considering changing the production volumes, as in the above example. The disadvantages of marginal costing are that it concentrates on the variable costs and only tells us whether we would be better off by accepting a contract at a certain price. It does not concern itself with the overheads or fixed costs, which might be much too high.

TOTAL ABSORPTION COSTING

Total absorption costing is a costing system that spreads the fixed costs out over the range of products or services of a company. Because all of the fixed costs are allocated in this way and added to the variable costs of each product or batch, all of the costs are 'absorbed'. This means that, providing the prices of the products or services are set so that they cover the total costs, and enough are sold, then the company must make a profit. The danger with this system comes from the fact that assumptions must be made about the future volumes, and if sales and/or production fall below these volumes then not all of the costs will be absorbed.

To overcome this problem a company can use a graph to identify the level of sales/production necessary to cover the costs at certain prices.

In the example in figure 4.2 the variable costs per cost unit are £5 and the fixed costs are £1,000 per week. The graph covers the range up to 400 cost units, which is the most it could produce without increasing the fixed costs by renting more space etc.

The horizontal axis shows the number of cost units produced and the vertical axis shows the total cost per unit. The plots have been calculated by dividing the fixed costs by the various production volumes and adding the variable cost of £5.

For example, for the plot for 200 units:

Fixed costs £1,000 divided by production of 200 =	£5
Plus variable costs	£5
	—
Total costs	10

In figure 4.2 the curve represents the break-even point at the various production volumes. If less is charged then losses will result.

Both marginal and absorption costing have their uses in a business. It is up to the Cost Accountant or Management Accountant, or

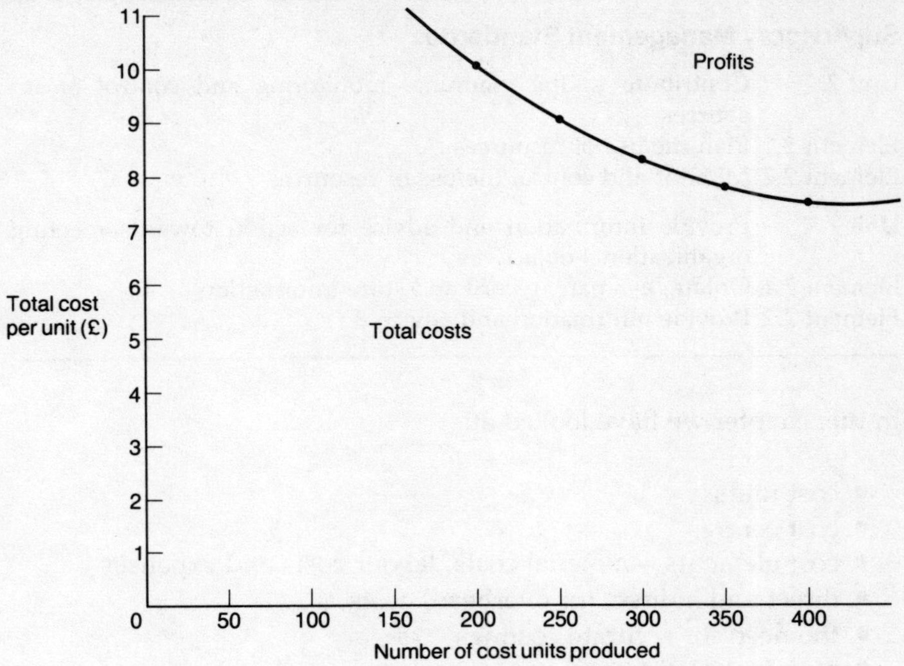

Figure 4.2 Break-even chart – total absorption costing

whoever is covering the role, to make sure that adequate accurate costing data has been collected to be able to respond to the needs of the business for information to fuel its decision making.

SUMMARY

The need for controlling costs should be very apparent to anyone in a supervisory/front line management position. However, what is not always obvious is the actual cost to the business or organization of certain materials, overtime and equipment. It is not always understood that the business might be paying high interest rates on overdrafts relating to the excess stocks it is holding. The cost of having to do work again because it was wrong the first time also is not always appreciated. All supervisors/front line managers have a role to play in helping to bring down costs, and units 2 and 7 can be applied to this.

Supervisory Management Standards:

Unit 2	Contribute to the planning, monitoring and control of resources
Element 2.1	Plan the use of resources
Element 2.2	Monitor and control the use of resources
Unit 7	Provide information and advice for action towards meeting organizational objectives
Element 7.1	Obtain, evaluate, record and store information
Element 7.2	Provide information and advice

In this chapter we have looked at:

- cost units
- cost centres
- cost elements – material costs, labour costs and expenses
- direct and indirect (or overhead) costs
- the need for accurate costings
- marginal costing
- fixed and variable costs
- contribution
- break-even point
- break-even charts
- profit/volume ratio
- total absorption costing

FURTHER READING

John Arnold and Tony Hope, *Accounting for Management Decisions*, 2nd edn. Prentice Hall, 1990.

Graham Mott, *Accounting for Non-Accountants*, 3rd edn. Kogan Page, 1990.

Alan Pizzey, *Cost and Management Accounting*, 3rd edn. P.C.P., 1990.

Chapter 5

How Are We Doing?

Supervisory Management Standards	
Unit 2	Contribute to the planning, monitoring and control of resources
Element 2.2	Monitor and control the use of resources
Unit 7	Provide information and advice for action towards meeting organizational objectives
Element 7.1	Obtain, evaluate, record and store information

In chapter 2 we decided that one of the main reasons for keeping accounts is to see whether or not the business is trading profitably. However, whilst our profit and loss statement will enable us to calculate how much profit we have made, it does not help us to identify how much we should have made from the resources we have employed. Similarly, the balance sheet will tell us how much of the working capital at one given date is tied up in raw materials, work in progress, finished goods and debtors, but how do we know if it is too much or too little, and is the amount we owe our creditors unreasonable? How can we compare one year's trading results against another year's, other than by looking at the profit made? Also, if we are able to obtain the balance sheet and accounts of our major competitor, how can we see how their figures compare with our own?

The answer to the above question lies in the use of **ratio analysis**.

A ratio, as we will discuss later in the 'Managing Information' section, expresses the relationship between two amounts to enable comparisons to be drawn from them. The results are expressed either as fractions or, more normally, in the format x:y (here we would say 'x to y'). For example, if we wanted to relate the amount of work that came from Wells (Plumbers) Ltd commercial work to the domestic work in a year, and the figures were £120,000 commercial and £60,000 domestic, we would express it as being in the ratio of 2:1 (2 to 1). Obviously, other ways of expressing the situation would be by saying that the income from commercial work was twice that of the domestic, or that the domestic work income was only half that of the commercial. Where the ratio format would be particularly useful is if we were comparing Wells (Plumbers) Ltd with a similar plumbing company where the ratio might be 4:1. This would indicate that the commercial work income was four times the amount of the domestic work income. From our earlier considerations on budgets and cash flow it could suggest that the commercial work was more profitable but that still more working capital was tied up as debtors.

In ratio analysis in finance, where we are looking at business performance, we often express our results in percentage form. This is not strictly correct in terms of ratios. Sometimes when looking at stock levels it is more convenient to calculate it as so many days or so many weeks of stock. Debtors and creditors figures expressed as so many days of credit given or taken can be far more meaningful than using the correct ratio format.

We can calculate ratios in finance and the running of the business in hundreds of instances, and in 'Managing Information' we will discuss ratios you might want to set up to help you monitor and control your unit of responsibility. At this point in time, however, it will be best if we look at just a few of the most important ratios that enable us to analyse and compare the financial performance of two companies in the same line of business, or the same company over two accounting periods.

The ratios we are going to look at fall into four different categories:

1 Profitability ratios
2 Liquidity ratios
3 Use of Assets ratios
4 Capital ratios

1. PROFITABILITY RATIOS

1.1 Return on capital employed

This is undoubtedly the most important comparison between the results of different companies. It is the ratio which tells us how much has been earned during the year on the amount of capital invested in the company or business. We sometimes hear on the news on radio or television that one of our biggest companies has made over a billion pounds in profit during the previous year's trading. However, this isolated piece of information, which often appears to be a criticism, is meaningless without knowing the level of return that it represents and the amount of capital employed in the business. If we liken it to money we have in a building society in savings, and we receive £50 in interest on our deposit of £500, we would have received a return on our capital of 10%. The interest in this case is similar to the profit earned, and our deposit would be the same as the capital employed. If, on the other hand, we received £50 on a deposit of £1,000, our return would only have been 5% and we might feel that we could do better elsewhere. The same can be said of companies: should the company that made over a billion pounds really have made over two billion pounds in view of the amount of capital used in the company?

The **return on capital employed** (ROCE) is calculated using the following formula:

$$\text{ROCE} = \frac{\text{Operating Profit}}{\text{Capital Invested}} \times 100$$

Here the 'operating profit' or trading profit is defined as being that which arises purely out of the operational activities of a business, and excludes any non-opertional income or expenditure, such as loan interest, investment income or profit from the sale of fixed assets, and is taken before the deduction of interest and tax payments. The 'capital invested' figure is as at the start of the trading year and includes the shareholders' funds plus any loan capital. The test here is would the shareholders be better off selling the business and putting the money into something else, e.g. a building society account?

1.2 Gross margin

This is our 'mark-up' on what it has cost us to produce the goods if we are manufacturers, or to buy the goods for resale if we are retailers.

$$\text{Gross Margin \%} = \frac{\text{Gross Profit}}{\text{Sales Income}} \times 100$$

The gross profit represents the sales income less the direct cost of those sales, and therefore has to be enough to cover all of the company's overheads and pay the dividends as well as provide sufficient retained profits for future expansion. It therefore follows that if the gross margin is too small we must either increase income by increasing the volume of sales or the price, or by reducing overheads.

2 CASH OR LIQUIDITY RATIOS

2.1 Current ratio

$$\text{Current ratio} = \frac{\text{Current Assets}}{\text{Current Liabilities}}$$

This measures the ability of a company to pay its bills and is calculated by dividing the current assets by the current liabilities. By 'current' we mean receivable or payable within twelve months. Current assets should normally exceed current liabilities, and the ratio should normally be in the range 1.5 : 1 to 2.5 : 1, but this will depend on the business it is in, to some extent. Usually too low a ratio would indicate an 'over-trading' situation, where risks are being taken with the payment of bills. Too high a ratio would indicate inefficiency in the use of the company's assets: for example, the holdings of raw materials might be too high. Obviously much will depend on the sort of business the company is engaged in, as the faster the turnover of stock the more readily it converts into cash. The 'quality' of the debtors will also be important, and by quality in this case we are referring to how likely they are to be able to pay. If the ratio is too low we would have to look very carefully at the reason. For example, it might well be that a large part of the current liabilities figure relates to the repayment of a bank loan which is due in ten months time and which at that time could be renewed for a much longer period. If that were the case, the company would not have the cash flow problem that the ratio suggests.

By the expression 'over-trading' we mean that the company has expanded its sales too rapidly without taking account of whether its cash flow can cope with the additional money being tied up in increased working capital, like the stock and debtors.

2.2 Acid test (or quick ratio)

$$\text{Quick ratio} = \frac{\text{Current Assets} - \text{Stock}}{\text{Current Liabilities}}$$

This is very similar to the current ratio, but only uses a figure for current assets that are thought to be quickly realizable. This is usually achieved by deducting the figures for stock in case it is 'work in progress' or obsolete finished goods that will not sell. If the current assets used in this case turn out to be lower than the current liabilities it may not be cause for concern, but will need investigating carefully, and will certainly require a cash flow forecast.

2.3 Credit given (number of days)

$$\text{Credit Given} = \frac{\text{Average Debtors Figure for the Year}}{\text{Sales Income}} \times 365$$

This gives the company an indication of how quickly it is getting its money in. For internal purposes it should be calculated and plotted on a regular basis to identify trends. Where a large proportion of the sales go to a few customers, it might be necessary to divide the sales income up and calculate one or more ratios for the large customers and one for the remainder. Whilst the formula calls for the average yearly figure for debtors to be used, to identify the overall picture the year-end figure may be the only one available, but do remember that this may not be typical. The number of days of credit given by the company (or taken by its customers) may be based on an agreed figure of (say) 30 days, but it will be important to see how the overall figure for debtors varies from this.

2.4 Credit Received (number of days)

$$\text{Credit Received} = \frac{\text{Average Creditors Figure for the Year}}{\text{Purchases}} \times 365$$

Obviously this is a measure of how quickly the company is paying its suppliers. The comments above for credit given largely apply here also. This would be of particular importance to anyone who is owed money by the company, such as a supplier or bank. It could also be of interest to a prospective customer who wanted to be sure that the company was not about to go out of business.

3 USE OF ASSETS RATIOS

3.1 Stock-holding ratios

Finished goods (expressed in weeks of sales):

$$\frac{\text{Stock of Finished Goods}}{\text{Sales}} \times 52$$

The levels of stocks of finished goods have been changing for several years as a result of the 'just in time' concept and as a result of changes in work practice which enable greater flexibility. For all companies and organizations who buy in goods, services and components the move has been towards smaller orders and deliveries and very much lower levels of stock held, including reserves of stock held by retailers. This can only work if their suppliers, including the manufacturers of the goods, can respond rapidly to their restocking requirements. If manufacturers cannot produce goods quickly and in relatively small quantities, they have to maintain increased stocks of finished goods themselves. We are therefore seeing a movement in stock-holding values from the end-users and their immediate suppliers to some of the manufacturers. Many manufacturers will be able to improve their responsiveness by speeding up the resetting of their machines to enable them to change from one product to another more quickly. This will make it possible to produce goods in smaller batches and will enable them to reduce stocks, both of finished goods and work in progess.

> **THINK POINT**
>
> If you are *In Charge* of any sort of store, even if it is no more than the stationery cupboard, ask yourself how much money is tied up in that stock and how much it could be reduced by.

3.2 Raw materials (expressed in weeks of purchases)

$$\frac{\text{Stock of Raw Materials}}{\text{Purchases}} \times 52$$

There is a tendency in many of us to be somewhat squirrel-like in the sense that we hoard goods and like to be sure that we are not going to run out. This applies to stocks of both finished goods and raw materials. The person responsible for ordering certain stocks may be quite junior and will not necessarily realize what his or her actions can cost. Overstocking may be done with the best of intentions in order to prevent the company or organization from running out. This happens in all sorts of situations – from the person in charge of the cash in a supermarket who holds too much change, to the office junior who orders enough notebooks to last five years. The ordering and control process is covered in the *In Charge* book on *Managing Operations*, but the financial cost of the stock and the cost of space taken up by excess stock is our concern here.

3.3 Stock turnover ratio (finished goods)

$$\text{Stock Turnover} = \frac{\text{Cost of Sales}}{\text{Average Stocks Held}}$$

This will vary enormously between different types of business, from a supermarket to a builders merchant. Too low a turnover for the type of business involved could result in damaged or outdated, and therefore unsaleable, stock.

3.4 Fixed asset ratios

$$\frac{\text{Sales Income}}{\text{Fixed Assets}}$$

This is expressed as the number of times the total of fixed assets go into the sales income, but could also be expressed in the form that each £1 of fixed assets created £X of sales. It is a measure of the ability of the management to use the assets of the company to generate sales. This will obviously depend on the type of business, but is useful as a comparison from year to year or between companies operating in the same line of business.

Where it can fall down is the fact that the figures for fixed assets may be historic. The conventional way of arriving at the historical figures for fixed assets is to take the original purchase price and deduct the accumulated depreciation to date. For example, if the company had land and buildings purchased ten years ago, then it is extremely unlikely that the balance sheet figure would bear any resemblance to the actual value. To make this ratio more meaningful, it would be necessary to arrive at a valuation for the fixed assets and to use that.

4 CAPITAL RATIOS

4.1 Turnover of capital

$$\frac{\text{Sales Income}}{\text{Capital Employed}}$$

The comments and example above under 'fixed assets' apply equally here. Any difference between the balance sheet value of the fixed assets and the actual value would result in an increase in the amount of capital by way of reserves. Profit is dependent on sales, so this ratio highlights the ability of the management to generate sales from the capital at their disposal. It is not possible to give guidelines as to what this should ideally be, as it will vary from industry to industry. Its importance therefore comes from comparisons made within the same company for different accounting periods, and between companies in the same type of business.

4.2 Gearing

$$\text{Gearing \%} = \frac{\text{Loan Capital}}{\text{Share Capital} + \text{Reserves}} \times 100$$

This ratio, expressed as a percentage, calculates the relationship between shareholders' funds (share capital plus reserves) and money borrowed for periods longer than one year. If a company is too reliant on borrowed money on which it has to pay interest annually, it risks liquidation during adverse trading years if it cannot pay the interest and repayments. Like the last two ratios we have looked at, the historic value of the fixed assets might cause the shareholders' funds to need adjusting to make this more meaningful.

Many of the ratios we have looked at will not necessarily apply to your job at this stage, but will give you an insight into how a business works and an understanding of some more of the language used. The stock ratios in particular may be relevant, so do make use of them.

SUMMARY

Supervisory Management Standards:

Unit 2	Contribute to the planning, monitoring and control of resources
Element 2.2	Monitor and control the use of resources
Unit 7	Provide information and advice for action towards meeting organizational objectives
Element 7.1	Obtain, evaluate, record and store information

In this chapter we have looked at the use of ratio analysis as a guide to how well a business is doing.

We have looked at performance ratios on profitability, use of assets, cash or liquidity, and capital adequacy, but have made the proviso that we must be careful that the historic figures for fixed assets in the balance sheets do not distort our results.

Chapter 6

Compensation and Payment Systems

Supervisory Management Standards	
Unit 2	Contribute to the planning, monitoring and control of resources
Element 2.1	Plan the use of resources
Element 2.2	Monitor and control the use of resources
Unit 7	Provide information and advice for action towards meeting organizational objectives
Element 7.2	Provide information and advice

Instead of calling this chapter 'Wages and Payment Systems', which is the more normal way in this country, we have deliberately chosen the expression 'Compensation'. Compensation, which means balance or recompense, is now being adopted by the human resources professionals (who used to be known as the personnel or staff department) to refer to all of the different payments and benefits given to employees. If we think of a pair of old-fashioned scales, on one side we have input by the employees, and this should be balanced on the other by the payments and benefits they receive from the employer.

In figure 6.1 we have used a variety of different payments and benefits that would fit into our definition of compensation, but we can see also that on the other side we have recognized that employees give more than just their direct work. All too often when a job is advertised people only look at the basic wages or salary. When we are offered a job or a promotion few of us think to negotiate any additional benefits or try to substitute some for others, and yet with many employers this would be possible.

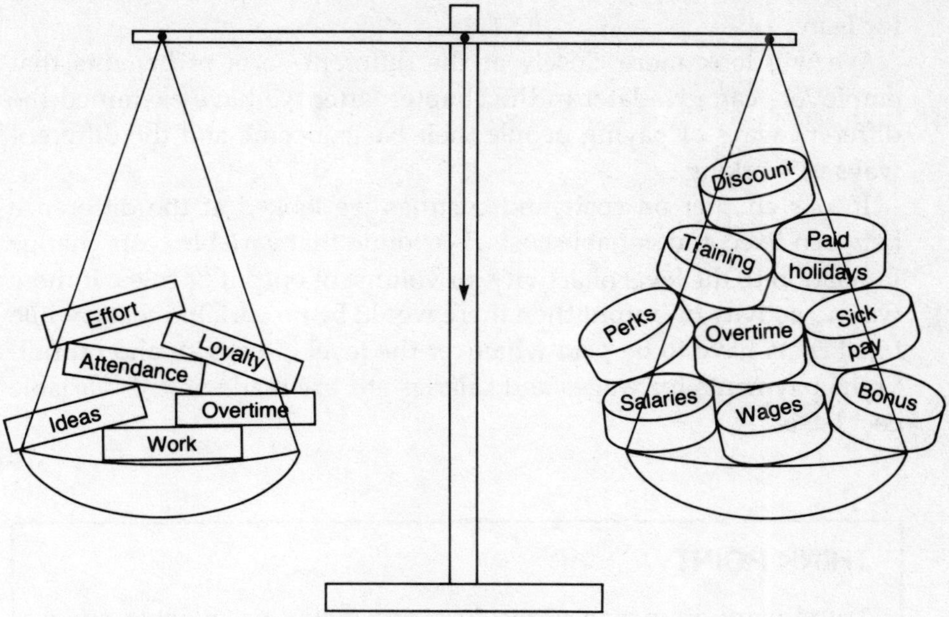

Figure 6.1 The balance of work and effort with pay and benefits

For example, at the start of *In Charge, Managing People* we met Jean, who had just been promoted by her boss, Mr Raymond, to the position of section supervisor. What if, before accepting the position, she had asked Mr Raymond that as part of the 'compensation package' she could attend a course at the local college on supervisory management at the employer's expense. At worst Mr Raymond might say no, but this is not all that likely as nearly all employers have a training budget. He might say that he would have to arrange it with the training officer, or if the training budget was used up for the year, make a note for her to attend the following year. Most employers would be pleased that she wanted to become more efficient in her new job and be glad that she had raised the subject. Jean would gain confidence from the knowledge received and from contact with others who were in a similar position to herself, as well as the qualification. Whether her employer would be able to release her from work to attend the course during the daytime, or whether she would have to attend during evenings, could be another area of negotiation. Persuading her employer to pay for her qualification would be an additional benefit, and whilst in this case it would also be a benefit to the employer as well, it could form part of the compensation package for Jean.

We will look more closely at the different sorts of benefits that employers can give later in the chapter, after we have examined the different ways of paying people their basic income and the different ways of working.

In our chapter on costs and costings we looked at the difference between fixed and variable costs. We found that variable costs change in relation to the level of activity, or volume of output or sales. If there was no activity or output then there would be no variable costs, while fixed costs have to be paid whatever the level of activity and output. Some payments for wages and salaries etc. are made on this variable cost basis.

THINK POINT

Try to work out which of the following would be variable costs and which would be fixed costs.

Piecework

Piecework is one of the best examples of what is generally referred to as 'payment by results'. In this system workers are paid in relation to the number of items they have produced, packed etc. It has a long history and is still widely used where the work is repetitive, set rates can be agreed and the number of items can be easily checked. It is therefore used in some factories and, for obvious reasons, is the usual method of paying home-workers. It also is used in businesses which have a large proportion of casual labour, such as fruit and hop picking. Payment rates can be stepped so that higher rates can be earned by those who achieve the higher levels of output, but this depends on the needs of the business. In factories this system depends very much on agreeing levels of output which are accepted by all as being fair. Here the accurate measurement of work as advocated by F. W. Taylor in his *Principles of Scientific Management* is particularly important (see *In Charge, Managing People*). In the past this has often led to disputes, but the greatest disadvantage in today's business climate is that quality suffers in the need to achieve maximum output (see *In Charge, Managing Operations*).

Time rates

The vast majority of employees are paid on a time rate system. They may be paid by the hour, by the day, by the week or by the month, but employers find the time rate system far easier to administer. From the employee's point of view it does give a regular payment which is easily understood, although the more experienced workers can be demotivated by the fact that they receive the same as workers who are new to the job. In terms of quality, as the system provides no incentive to hurry the worker is able to concentrate on achieving a higher standard. However, it is necessary to have much greater levels of supervision to prevent lateness, absenteeism and time wasting, and to encourage output – and this can be costly. Many employees resent the need for clocking on and off, particularly where the system is only applied to production workers and is not used by the office staff and management.

Measured day work

In this system each operator is usually put into a payment band which relates to his or her normal level of output per day. If the operator demonstrates that he or she can produce more by frequently producing the levels required by the next band, they can be promoted to that band and will receive the higher daily rate of pay of that band. Similarly, if an operator frequently falls below the daily rate for their band, they can be moved down to a lower band where less output will be expected of them, but they will receive a lower daily rate of pay. This system obviously is intended to combine the benefits of the piecework system, and its incentive to produce more, with the ease of administration of the timework system. Unfortunately it does sometimes produce the wrong attitude in the workforce. Because the operators see themselves as being paid for a certain daily quota they are likely to slow down or stop work as soon as they have achieved it. This can be a serious problem for the management when, for example, they have an urgent order to fill. Also, where continual minor improvements to the methods of working as a result of quality circles or improvement groups (see *In Charge, Managing Operations*) lead to increased output, it is often difficult to get workers amicably to accept changes to the required output bands. On the other hand, the desire to progress to higher bands can be motivated by the need for achievement, recognition and social acceptance rather than the money (see motivation in *Managing People*).

Group schemes

So far we have looked at systems which have either an incentive to produce more or an ease of administration from a payroll point of view. There are many variations on the above systems to try to obtain the benefits of both incentive and ease of administration, and different companies and industries have adapted them to suit their own circumstances. This is certainly the case where one job is dependent on another or others to be able to produce at a given rate. For example, if worker D cannot do her part of the process until workers A, B and C have each done theirs, we can easily see that it only requires one of them to work at a slower speed and those after them in the process will be restricted to the pace of the slowest. Often in this sort of situation the employer will operate a **group piecework** or **bonus** system, where a rate is set for each group or team of workers. For this to operate efficiently the number in the group needs to be restricted to not more than eight, and much will depend on the ability and personality of the team leader, and the make-up of the group in terms of age, experience etc. Training in leadership skills for team leaders can be important in these cases, as can teamwork training for the group.

Bonus schemes

Bonus schemes are additional to basic salary or wages and are intended as incentives and rewards. We have already looked at circumstances where operators can earn additional money or bonus by achieving output in excess of certain agreed norms. This can be applied to other sorts of measurable results as well. Examples of these would include sales and marketing, where the level of bonus or commission is directly related to the results obtained. In *Managing People* we discussed appraisal schemes and the setting of goals: the reward for achieving or surpassing those goals is often a clearly defined bonus arrangement which can amount to as much as 30 per cent of salary. However, it would be very time consuming to set goals for all employees, and indeed would be almost impossible for some jobs.

Bonus schemes can be based on whole units rather than individual achievement, and many factory-wide schemes are in operation. The advantages of these are that they encourage the workforce to identify more with the objectives of the management and take more of an interest in the business. However, the larger the factory the more impersonal it can become. It is then more difficult to identify with and feel an important part of the unit, and with this in mind some companies in the United States try to limit each production unit to no more than a hundred people. The obvious disadvantage with this type of incentive scheme is that the reward is somewhat removed from the efforts and output of the individual. The advantages are that those employees who are not involved in production, such as the clerical staff who may work just as hard, can also benefit. These schemes require very comprehensive costing arrangements, and information on costs and results must be freely available to the workforce.

Overtime

Overtime can be a very efficient means of evening out the peaks and troughs of work levels. Because of its uncertain nature and unsociable hours it is usally paid at a higher rate than normal hours, although some job agreements do guarantee a certain amount of overtime. Apart from where guaranteed levels exist, overtime provides a flexible labour resource for use as and when required, and often saves having to recruit and pay additional time rate employees. The disadvantages of using overtime regularly to cover excess work-load include the fact that the increased hours and income quickly become the norm, and work is spread out to cover the increased period of time (the system is open to abuse). Also there are only so many hours that each individual can work efficiently, so for much of the overtime the worker is operating at below normal level of output. Management experts in other European countries have criticized the often excessive hours worked by managers and workers in this country because of the fall-off in productivity occasioned by working too many hours.

Profit sharing

Profit-sharing schemes operate in a variety of ways and are usually paid on an annual basis. They are often paid in shares rather than cash by companies who are quoted on the stock market. They are directly linked to the level of profit earned by the company, which must allow for sufficient funds to be retained in the business to pay the annual dividend to shareholders. The payment in shares rather than cash is a definite advantage to the company as it preserves the company's cash resources. In cases where a share scheme is approved by the Inland Revenue the shares do not attract income tax, providing they are held for five years. If they are sold before the five years are up income tax is payable at a rate which is dependent on how long they have been owned. Where profit sharing is paid in cash it attracts income tax in the normal way.

SALARY STRUCTURES

Salaries have their origin in the Latin word *salarium*, which was the salt money paid to Roman soldiers. Now they are monthly payments, made under an annually agreed rate of pay, to attract, recruit, retain and reward employees.

The overall salary structure within a company or organization will depend on its salary policy, culture and objectives. For example, if its objective is to be the best and most prestigious in its field it needs to attract, recruit and retain the best employees available. In this case the salary policy of the company will be to pay the top market rates in the various fields. Alternatively, if the objective is to maximize profit by running a cut-price operation, the opposite will apply. Much will depend on the market the company or organization is operating in, and the prevailing market conditions and rates.

The identification of a definite salary policy and a salary structure is extremely important. Without them there will be a tendency for all sorts of imbalances to be created as a result of reacting to situations, and these in turn will create disharmony and result in staff turnover. For example, if a company whose chairman is the most dominant director needs a new finance manager, he or she might persuade the rest of the board that the position is so important that they must pay near the top of the market range to attract the right person. Conversely, he or she might decide that the sales manager's job is far less important and so should be recruited at a salary which is at the lower end of the market range for that job. The results of these two decisions could be far-reaching. The finance manager could be on a very similar salary to the managing director and could see her/himself as an equal, whereas the sales manager would be seen as being in a lower level of management. If the sales manager is paid at the lowest part of the range for sales managers, the same will apply to the remainder of the sales force, and this in time will result in a low quality or inexperienced sales team which has a high staff turnover. The ripples created by these two decisions could affect the whole company. You can imagine the sort of departmental team the new finance manager would gradually put together and the sort of power that the department would wield within the company. The market salary range for company accountants is different from that for sales managers, which is different from personnel managers, production managers etc. If the company had decided on a salary policy of paying, say, just above the mid-point of the market rates for all jobs, the above situation would have been avoided.

In order to develop its salary structure, a company or organization will need to analyse the content of all of its jobs and evaluate the level of importance of each component part. It might decide to carry out this process itself if it is large enough; or, alternatively, employ a company that specializes in this work. If an expert company is employed they will be able to advise on the salary ranges paid for the various equivalent jobs in the market and on how different jobs are usually ranked in terms of importance and payment. This information will help the company to decide upon its salary grades and on what basis increases will be awarded. Obviously this process will need to involve the trade unions wherever they are recognized.

The whole salary and wages structure in any organization is like a giant jigsaw puzzle. Situations where people turn down promotion because it will involve them in loss of take-home pay need to be avoided wherever possible. How would Jean feel on taking up her promotion to find that she had to supervise people who earned more than she did? In our example of the company that recruited a new finance manager and a new sales manager, what would the salesmen and saleswomen feel if clerks in the finance office received higher salaries than they did – how valued would they feel?

The salary structure is likely to be based on the following three main types, or could be made up of a combination of them:

1 age related
2 graded
3 progression curves

Age related

This structure is very simple in that it has a salary for a particular age, and progression can be by age alone (see figure 6.2). This can obviously be very demotivating, so very often each age has a small range to enable higher payments to be made to reward those who have demonstrated higher levels of performance. As this becomes progressive and there is a need to continue to reward someone who performs well each year, the range at each age has to become wider. As a result of changes in our society starting in the 1960s, this structure nowadays tends to be limited to those under the age of 21 years, whereas before that it was used for employees up to the age of 30 and beyond.

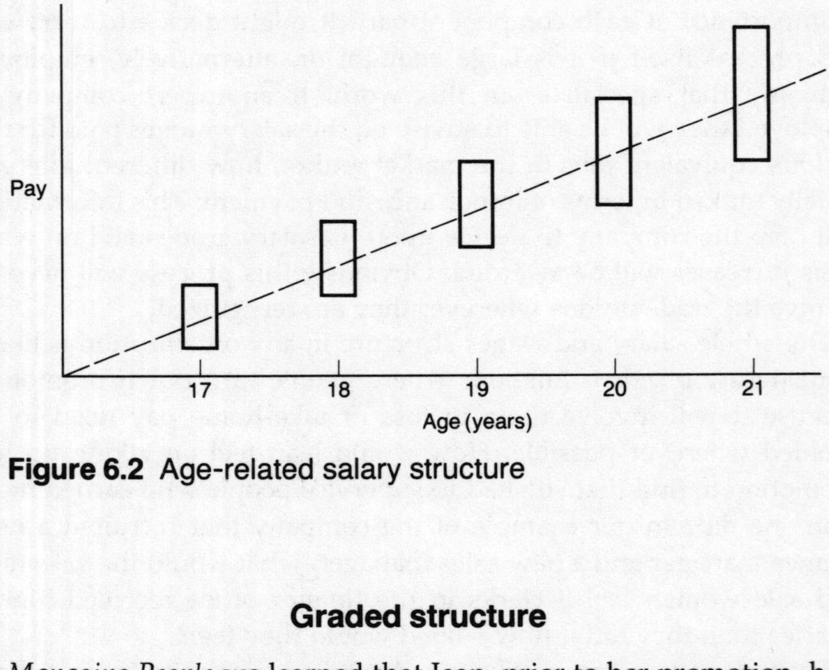

Figure 6.2 Age-related salary structure

Graded structure

In *Managing People* we learned that Jean, prior to her promotion, held a scale three position with her local authority employer, and that her new supervisory responsibilities were at scale five. These are examples of a graded structure. All of the jobs, after they have been evaluated as to content, are put into a 'pecking-order', usually as a result of allocating points for the importance of the different parts of the job and adding them up. The range of jobs, from the most important to the most junior, is then divided into bands or grades and a range of salaries is allocated to each grade. Each grade needs to have maximum and minimum salaries so that the higher levels of performance can be rewarded. If we return to the case of Jean, as a scale three she was probably on the maximum for her grade because she was considered to be suitable for promotion to scale five. In view of the fact that she was jumping scale four, she would probably start her new job at or near the bottom of scale five. Figure 6.3 makes this a bit easier to understand.

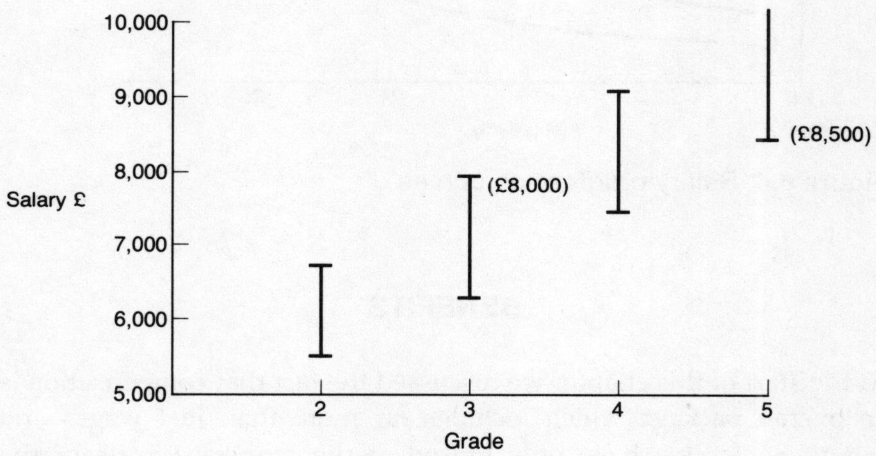

Figure 6.3 Graded salary structure

Progression curves

A salary progression curve seeks to link appropriate salary to age and experience over a period of several years (see figure 6.4). It has to pay close attention to the rates in the marketplace for similar jobs to identify the level that fits in with the company's or organization's salary policy. It must also fit in with overall company salary structure, but often will include provision for rewarding higher performance and greater starting qualifications. This sort of structure only covers the first few years of employment.

After that, an individual will find an appropriate level in the graded system, if there is one, or be on performance-related pay or receive percentage increases in salary annually.

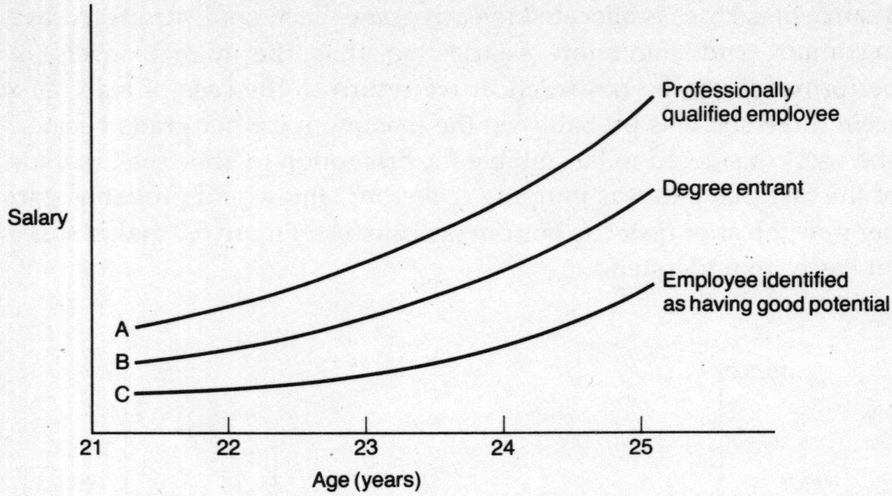

Figure 6.4 Salary progression curves

BENEFITS

At the start of this chapter we discussed the fact that compensation is an overall package which includes far more than just wages and salary. So far we have only looked at the monetary parts of the package – wages, salary, overtime, bonus, commission and profit sharing – but almost all jobs nowadays have valuable benefits included in the compensation package. Once upon a time these were referred to as 'fringe benefits', but they are now seen as an integral part of the total remuneration or compensation package.

Pensions

Pensions are probably the most important benefit: they represent a deferred wage or salary that has been earned. Unfortunately they are also extremely complex and at the time when most of us are starting work they are far from our thoughts. It is only when we are nearing retirement age that we start to become interested in them, and that can be much too late. Most companies and organizations believe that their employees should receive more than just a minimum level of pension. They can choose to remain within the earnings-related part of the state system – known as SERPS, the State Earnings-Related Pension

Scheme – or contract their employees out of it. In order to contract out the company's or organization's own scheme must be approved by the Inland Revenue. The scheme must provide for a guaranteed minimum pension (GMP) which is revalued in line with inflation. Where a company scheme is approved, the employer will be able to claim tax relief on the contributions it makes to the pension fund and on the pension administration expenses. Pension arrangements are complex, however, and need expert advice, particularly with regard to investing the funds. Some pension schemes have a contributory element which requires each employee to pay in a percentage of their gross pay each week or month, related to their basic wage or salary.

Although we have talked in terms of the company or organization setting up and contributing to the pension scheme, it is important to remember that the funds of a pension scheme must not be controlled by the company. Funds must either be deposited with a life insurance company or be set up as a trust fund which will be controlled by trustees. The trustees may be individuals who have been voted in by the employees and existing pensioners, with some elected by the company, or specialist trustee companies who are subsidiaries of banks etc. The trustees are responsible for the pension funds and ensure that the rules relating to them are adhered to.

Employees who leave to take another job now have the right to the pension with their old employer being preserved or transferred to the scheme of their new employer. Before deciding which of these options to adopt it is best to find out as much as possible about the relative performances of the two schemes.

Paid holidays

After pensions this is probably the next most expensive benefit in terms of cost to the employer. The average paid holiday per employee has increased over the last twenty-five years, so that the average in this country is now over three weeks plus bank holidays, with managers receiving between four and six weeks. Many companies insist on holidays only being taken during the annual factory shutdown periods of two weeks in the summer and one week at Christmas. In other cases where there is no shutdown, strict control is maintained to ensure that adequate staff are always available to meet the company's needs. This can sometimes result in the most junior members of staff having to choose between taking their main holiday either in April or October. The paid holidays of schoolteachers are one instance in which the general public recognizes the total package concept of compensation. In this case any of the teaching unions' major salary claims are quickly dismissed by the majority of the public on the grounds of the number and length of school holidays that should be taken into account when assessing remuneration.

Sick Pay

Sick pay is sometimes taken for granted by the workforce but represents another extremely costly benefit. One of the tests by which society judges how good an employer is relates to how it treats a sick employee. Because of this social pressure most sick-pay schemes are quite generous, and even after the maximum time on full pay has been taken schemes usually have some arrangement whereby someone senior within the company can authorize an extension.

Obviously the above is designed to help employees cope with a long illness or accidental injury etc., but the most costly aspect of paid sickness are the short periods of self-certificated sickness. All too often these are abused, and patterns can be traced where some employees are only sick either side of weekends and holidays. This has become known as 'Friday/Monday syndrome'. This absenteeism, for that is what it is, needs controlling by those of us who are In Charge. The remainder of the workforce is usually fully aware of what is happening and will be watching us to see what action we are going to take. Some companies and organizations have an allowance of so many days self-certificated sickness per employee per year, but this tends to be seen as a right to that many days off whether the employee is sick or not. Obviously, where people are employed on a piecework basis, or only receive the statutory sick pay, absenteeism is not usually a problem. A number of smaller companies are now being forced to abandon their sick-pay schemes just to be able to stay in business.

So far we have looked at pensions, holidays and sick pay, and against each we have commented on the fact that they are very costly to the employer. What we need to do now to put it into perspective is to discuss just how much they cost. Pension schemes of the non-contributory sort vary according to the package that has been set up, but can be as high as twenty per cent of an individual's salary. The production lost through closing down for three weeks holiday each year is obviously enormous, bearing in mind that only the variable costs stop during this time. In other companies and organizations where they do not shut down and employees all take their holidays at different times, a number of additional staff are necessary to cover for holidays and sickness. These may not be a designated relief staff, but the content of the jobs needs to allow a certain amount of slack to cover these occasions. If we allow an average of seventeen working days per employee per year for holidays (which is about the average), plus six to ten days for sickness, depending on the business they are in, the total is twenty-three to twenty-seven days. In a company working a five-day week that effectively amounts to employing an extra worker for every nine jobs. Think what that could amount to in Jean's local authority employer, which has several thousands of employees. In the past we might have said, 'well, they can afford it', but recent experience has taught us that costs can only be reduced so far as a result of improved technology and performance before jobs have to go. This is not to suggest that we have all got to give up our holidays, pensions and sick pay etc. to remain in a job, but merely to remind us that they are an integral part of the cost of employing people. Overall the provision of benefits can add up to thirty per cent to the wages and salaries bill.

Uniforms and work wear

The number of employees who receive the benefit of having their uniform or work wear provided for them has expanded rapidly over the last ten years. The need for presenting a smart company image to the customer has resulted in banks, offices and shops adopting the sort of uniform previously associated with airlines. Also, in many factories, the Japanese idea that all employees, including the management, should be dressed the same in order to break down some of the social barriers, has increased the provision of work wear. The Health and Safety laws governing protective clothing have had a similar effect. Many people would not necessarily see this provision as a benefit until they calculate how much extra they would have to spend on clothes for work.

Subsidized food and drink

This is another widely provided benefit. It can include a subsidized in-company canteen or restaurant, luncheon vouchers, meal allowances when working off-site, subsidized drinks trolleys or machines, free tea and coffee making ingredients etc.

Discounts on goods and services

This heading again covers many different types of benefit. It includes the staff discounts that the big stores and other retailers give, the reduced rate mortgages and loans for banks, building society and insurance company staff, the cheap car schemes for the employees of the car manufacturers, cheap flights for airline personnel, cheap holidays for travel agents and many more. Here the cost to the employer is much less because, in the main, they are seeking at least to cover the variable costs of the goods or services, while the staff member would still have the benefit of not having to pay for a proportion of the overheads or the profit margin.

Company cars and car fuel

These are benefits which are widely provided at higher managerial levels. The provision of company cars tends to fall into two categories; status cars and high mileage user cars. Status cars are very much part of the compensation package, as they are provided to any manager who has reached a certain level in the company or organization, and little account is taken of their need. High mileage user cars, on the other hand, are very much provided as a business need. The individual may have a daily need to use a car for business purposes and the annual mileage may be very high. The maintenance and running costs, such as motor tax and insurance, are paid by the company for both categories; and fuel may be provided for all mileage, or a fuel allowance may be given only for business miles.

The fact that the vehicles relating to both categories of owners are available to them for private use is recognized by the Inland Revenue. The system of taxation for cars is based on the original market value, the size of the engine and the business mileage during the year. Where fuel is provided for all mileage, or where the fuel allowance for business mileage is above a certain level for the size of the engine, the Inland Revenue see this as a benefit and taxes it accordingly. In addition, the employer's portion of the National Insurance contributions has to include car and fuel benefits.

Private health care cover

The need to have key personnel fit and at work has prompted many employers to provide private health cover. There is an obvious business logic in paying to have someone treated when it is convenient to the business and returned to work with the minimum possible delay. It has, however, in many businesses become another status 'perk', and in many cases it has also been extended to cover the immediate families of the employees concerned. The Inland Revenue tax the provision of private health care cover as a benefit in kind.

There are many, many more benefits and 'perks' that we could list, and every industry and company seems to have its own variations of them. The important thing to remember is that nearly all of them represent a cost to the business. This can be a straight monetary cost, in the sense that money is being paid away; or an opportunity cost, as a result of loss of output through giving someone time off for some reason.

Case Note 5

Before Colin Wells became self-employed he and Sue had taken it for granted that they would have a holiday away each year. Some years it was a struggle to find the money to pay for accommodation in a guest house or small hotel, but they always managed it somehow or other.

After Colin was made redundant and became self-employed they faced an additional dilemma. Not only had they to find the cost of the holiday now, but they had to add to that the lost income whilst Colin was not working. The result of this was that for the first two years Colin did not take a proper holiday and contented himself with the bank holiday weekends, although even then he was called out for burst pipes etc. When Colin and Sue discussed this they came to the conclusion that the loss of income through Colin taking a holiday instead of working was very much the same as for Colin's old employers. The building company that Colin used to work for closed down for three weeks a year for holidays which, like Colin's case now, resulted in no income.

In a similar way Colin's attitude to days off sick underwent a change, even though he had always had a good record of attendance. He recognized that however bad a cold he had, he needed to go to work. He would have to be incapable even of getting out of bed before he would miss a day now that he was working for himself, as he could see what it cost him in lost income.

With regard to taking out a private pension plan, when Colin heard the cost each year, he was shocked, even though it could be set against the tax payable. The thought of having to pay over a thousand pounds a year for even a very small additional pension was something he had not expected, and he realized that it was another cost he would have to provide for, wherever possible, when quoting for work.

When Wells Plumbers Ltd expands sufficiently to employ others, Colin will then be faced with the situation of employees who will expect to take time off for sickness and be paid for holidays. No doubt it will be difficult for him to come to terms with this at first, but we can now see his point of view. Now we can calculate the total cost of the compensation package instead of thinking that the only cost to the business is the wage paid.

THINK POINT

List all of the benefits that are available or are paid to you and your colleagues, and try to work out what your compensation package is worth in total.

Cafeteria system

We have not moved to a position where employees can choose the make up of their salary or wages plus benefits package, that is, the make up of their compensation. Some senior executives do have this arrangement, under what is referred to as a 'cafeteria system'. In this system they are given a figure that their total package can cost, and they can then choose what they want to include in it. Obviously a system which results in a tailor-made package to suit the needs of the individual would be very popular with the employee, but would be very difficult and costly to administer.

SUMMARY

This chapter has looked at the cost of human resources in a business or organization. Both units 2 and 7 are relevant, and there is a need to take stock of what control and monitoring systems you have for sickness and holidays. To what extent are the pay arrangements to compensate the workers and to meet the needs of the business appropriate? What information do you provide to management on pay and benefits?

Supervisory Management Standards:

Unit 2	Contribute to the planning, monitoring and control of resources
Element 2.1	Plan the use of resources
Element 2.2	Monitor and control the use of resources
Unit 7	Provide information and advice for action towards meeting organizational objectives
Element 7.2	Provide information and advice

In this chapter we have introduced the concept of the compensation package.

We have looked at the possibility of an individual negotiating an additional benefit or swapping one benefit for another, particularly at the time of promotion.

The various ways of paying wages based on output or time worked have been compared, and we have looked at the need for a salary policy and salary structure.

The main benefits given in this country have been discussed. By using the case study of Colin Wells as a sole trader and of Wells Plumbers Ltd, we have tried to consider the effects on the business and the overall costs.

Chapter 7

The External Environment

Supervisory Management Standards	
Unit 2	Contribute to the planning, monitoring and control of resources
Element 2.1	Plan the use of resources
Element 2.2	Monitor and control the use of resources

It would be wrong if we left this section on finance without considering the wider economic, political and environmental issues that affect the businesses and organizations in which we work.

In examining the external environment we are going to structure it on the 'ripple effect'. If we think of the company or organization that you work for as being the centre, we will examine the factors that affect the business starting with the nearest ones, such as local competition, and gradually move further out until we are looking at world issues.

MARKETS AND COMPETITION

So far we have looked at the ways in which businesses and organizations are financed and how they operate to make the profits they require to stay in business and to expand. Much of their success or failure to do so will depend on the level of competition.

The perfect market

If companies operated in a perfect market economy there would be perfect competition, but this would have to include the following factors:

1. A large number of buyers and sellers of each particular item, so that no one could influence the price
2. Everyone would have full knowledge of all of the products and prices
3. The design, construction, delivery, back-up service etc. of all products of the same sort would be identical.
4. It would be possible to buy or sell any amount of the product at the market price

This situation cannot completely exist in any one market, although economists like to search for examples of near perfect markets, like some of the world markets in raw materials and grain. However, perfection does provide a basis against which markets can be judged.

Monopolies

If we examine the first of the requirements for a perfect market, that of a large number of buyers and sellers, we can all think of situations where there is only one supplier of goods or services. It might be on a very local level, where there is only one public house or shop in a village and the next one might be miles away. Or it might be on a national level, like the Post Office or British Telecom. This situation we would describe as a monopoly and it has obvious dangers with regard to overpricing and profiteering.

Oligopoly

As in the case of monopolies, similar dangers exist where there is more than one seller or provider but still too few to be regarded as fully competitive. This situation is called an oligopoly, and examples would include the high street banks, instant coffee, synthetic fibres and beer. In each case the market is dominated by a few very large companies.

The opposite to a monopolistic situation would be one where there were too many producers trying to sell too many goods. This can happen when markets shrink, as in times of recession. If market forces are allowed to take their course, the situation resolves itself by a number being squeezed out of business, until production and capacity are more in line with the market for the product or service.

Intervention

Sometimes market forces are not allowed this freedom due to governmental intervention. Examples of this would include the intervention prices paid to farmers under the Common Agricultural Policy (CAP) of the European Community. This encourages farmers to produce as much as possible. The EC recognizes that many European farmers would be unable to produce profitably at world prices and would go out of business. It therefore fixes a price at which it will buy the farmers' produce. If a farmer can sell his or her produce for more in the open market they will do so, but if not they will sell at the intervention price to the intervention agency of the EC. Non-EC countries are charged an import levy on produce coming into the EC, which puts their price above the intervention level.

Another example of governmental intervention is the financial support given to the national airlines of other countries when they are making losses, and the international fixing of seat prices. This results in passengers in Europe paying nearly double the amount for a flight in Europe to a similar one in the USA.

The second of the requirements for a perfect market demands perfect knowledge on the part of the purchasers. This means that they will know everything about the products and prices of all of the suppliers of the goods they may wish to purchase. In most cases this level of information would be overwhelming and counter-productive, but in limited markets it can be quite normal.

Marketing and advertising

Marketing and, in particular, advertising can make markets both more and less perfect. More in the sense that they provide information to potential customers to improve their knowledge of what is available; and less in the sense that they seek to persuade potential customers that their product or service is in some way superior and is differentiable from the competition.

> **THINK POINT**
>
> How perfect is the market for the product(s) and/or service(s) that your employer produces? Who are your main competitors? Does your advertising try to emphasize that your product or service is in some way different?

FACTORS OF PRODUCTION

In the world generally there are limited resources and unlimited demands for them. Each society has only a limited amount of land, labour and capital; these are known as the factors of production.

1 Land

The amount of land in this country would seem to be very fixed, but much has been reclaimed in recent years. The usage of land has become much more restrictive than it used to be. For example, now it would be very difficult to obtain planning permission to build a large factory in most parts of the country, and the extraction of minerals is becoming increasingly restricted. Other countries have far fewer people per square mile than we do, and in many cases are increasing their usable land by reclamation and deforestation.

2 Labour

The overall population of the UK, at about 57.5 millions (1991), is slowly increasing and is predicted to be just over 59 millions by the year 2001. Of these the labour force, which is made up of those in work and those who are registered as unemployed, will be about 28.9 millions. This again is a slight increase, and results from the higher percentage of women who return to work after having a family.

Of the total UK population, 19% are under the age of 15 years, and 15.7% are over the age of 65 years. These figures are very much in line with other developed countries, but are in marked contrast to nearly all of the Third World countries in Africa, Asia and South America. In these countries those under 15 years of age make up in the region of 35% to 48% of the population, and those over 65 years of age make up about 3%. The population increase in these countries is such that if present rates were to continue their populations would double in about 17 years. The size of the available labour forces of these countries is therefore increasing rapidly, and levels of unemployment are already very high.

3 Capital

In chapter 2 we looked at the places where businesses get their capital, and in particular we mentioned that the best place from which to obtain capital is from retained profits. If we then look on a global basis we can see that the main factor that separates the rich nations from the poor is capital. It is also easy to see how, by using that capital to produce further profits, the rich nations get richer and the poor nations become comparatively poorer.

Over the years the richer nations have contributed either directly, or to funds such as the World Bank, to help the poorer nations. However, the huge amounts of interest due on the debts owed by the Third World mainly to banks in the rich nations, is resulting in a net flow of money from the poor nations to the rich ones. (In 1989 the figure for Third World debt was estimated to be $700 billion!) Some countries, particularly those in Asia, are welcoming joint ventures in their countries between themselves and companies from the rich nations. This is a means of obtaining capital from Japan and the West to build local industries. Given the availability of land and low-cost labour, these joint ventures will be very difficult to compete with. The economies of Thailand, Malaysia, Singapore, Indonesia, South Korea, Taiwan and Hong Kong have made, and are making, rapid progress, and China is looking to be one of the leading financial powers by the year 2050.

GOVERNMENT

Local government

The lowest level of government in this country is the parish council in England and the community council in Wales and Scotland. These have little or no powers and are unlikely to affect the business community at all. This also applies to town councils, which have the same status as parish councils but have at some time been given the right to adopt a different title and to have a mayor instead of a chairman.

The first level of local government which is likely to affect businesses is the district council. These have responsibilities for planning, housing, recreation, and refuse collection, and for the collection of the local taxes. City and borough councils are in fact district councils which operate under a different name only.

County councils form the next tier, with responsibilities for education, police, fire etc. These were the old 'shire' or non-metropolitan counties. For the old Greater London Council and metropolitan counties these responsibilities were transferred to a mixture of metropolitan districts, London boroughs and joint boards.

Since 1989 local government services have been subject to 'compulsory competitive tendering', but nearly three-quarters of the contracts have so far been won by the councils' own labour forces without any competition being offered. This situation is likely to change with the continued pressure by central government for greater efficiency.

Central government

Central government in this country is made up of the legislature, the judiciary, the executive and the civil service.

The legislature or lawmaking part is Parliament, which is made up of the Queen, the House of Lords and the House of Commons. However, we must also remember that many of our laws now come about as a result of our membership of the EC.

The judiciary is made up of our judges, who operate in the Queen's name. The House of Lords is the highest legal court in the country.

The executive is made up of the Prime Minister and the members of the cabinet. The cabinet is chosen by the Prime Minister and must obviously include the senior ministers. The executive decide on the government's policies and implement them.

The civil service is the administrative machine of government. Civil servants are servants of the Crown and are employed on a permanent basis, although they tend to be employed by particular departments. Each government department usually has a permanent secretary who is the adviser to the minister no matter which political party is in power. Although the permanent secretary in each department is very important and powerful it is the minister who is held accountable for the actions and policies of the department.

The role of government in the economy

Governments have a number of important economic functions and objectives to fulfil. These include the maintenance of full employment, price stability, the achievement of a high level of economic growth, the maintenance of a current account balance, the preservation of the environment and the overall balance of the distribution of wealth in our society. In addition to the above economic functions, the government has many other responsibilities, such as education, health, social security, transport and defence – all of which require it to collect and to spend money. These requirements are recognized by each of the political parties, but as the amount of money available from the different forms of taxation is always less than the demands for it, each political party will have different priorities for its use.

In chapter 3 we saw the need for using budgets to forecast the needs of a business in monetary and numerical terms for a trading period. The Chancellor of the Exchequer and the Treasury carry out this process for the country and monitor progress in much the same way. Each governmental department has its own budget, which is agreed with the Chancellor and the Treasury, and must abide by it. The decisions made by the Chancellor in conjunction with his cabinet colleagues can have important implications for all of us. These are not just related to whether cigarettes and alcohol are to be taxed more heavily, but include such things as the level of corporation tax which companies must pay on their profits, and the capital allowances on new plant and machinery. As we have already seen, these will affect how much profit will be retained in the business to make it grow.

The European Community

When we looked at central government in this country we identified four key parts: the legislature, the judiciary, the executive and the civil service. The EC has a similar four parts, but their structure and way of operating is, in some cases, very different.

The European Parliament consists of 518 members, or MEPs, of whom 81 are from the UK. Elections for the MEPs are held every five years, and in the Parliament they sit in their party political groups rather than their national ones. Unlike our national parliament, the European version has no powers to initiate or pass legislation, although it can and does make proposals for new laws to the European Commission. The role of the MEPs is to scrutinize and comment on new legislation before it is passed, and to represent the interests of their constituents. At present the Parliament is short of both authority and power.

The European Court of Justice is made up of judges from all of the community countries. It sits in Luxembourg and adjudicates on disputes arising from community laws which affect member states, institutions, companies or individuals. Member states can also request that it review the legality of acts of the Council of Ministers and the Commission.

The Council of Ministers is the equivalent of our executive or Cabinet, and is effectively the 'government' of the EC. It is made up of the appropriate minister from each of the member states according to the subject being discussed, and each member state assumes the presidency in turn for a period of six months. Final approval of new laws to be imposed throughout the EC is given by the Council of Ministers. Several times a year meetings are held which consist of the Prime Ministers and Heads of State.

The Commission is the equivalent of our civil service and is responsible for the day-to-day administration of the EC. It is headed by a president and seventeen commissioners, each of whom has a different area of responsibility. The commissioners are nominated by the member governments, two from each of the five largest countries and one from each of the other seven. The Commission drafts proposals for community laws, monitors the compliance of member states within the treaties, and implements community policies, such as the common agriculture policy (CAP). The Commission proposes new laws to control standards across the Community. Often these are seen as a threat to livelihoods or ways of life in one or more member states, and are highlighted by the media in the country concerned. Examples of these include the loss of some traditional cheeses because the system used to make them does not conform; or some small businesses going to the wall because they could not afford the equipment necessary to meet the new standards for their industry. It should, however, be emphasized that the Commission only proposes and drafts laws, it does not pass them.

THINK POINT

Who is your MEP and which party does he or she support?

THE ENVIRONMENT

The many issues associated with the environment are so enormous that most of us have the feeling there is little or nothing that we can do about it. The number of television programmes, magazine articles and stories of impending doom in the press have resulted in many people accepting that someone will have to do something. This situation has resulted in most people closing their minds to the subject, which in turn results in central government giving it a lower level of priority. One area where a substantial and growing minority have expressed interest is at local level, and most district councils have provided various recycling facilities. However, the main environmental problems cannot be solved simply by recycling bottles, paper and cans, although this does help to slow the deterioration of the situation.

The two main environmental problems are the destruction of the ozone layer and global warming. Both of these have been caused mainly by the developed countries, although they have only 25 per cent of the world's population. These then expect the Third World countries to forego the use of the cheap refrigerants and aerosol propellants that cause the destruction of the ozone layer, and to refrain from clearing the forests, which reduce the carbon dioxide that is the main cause of global warming. With their increasing populations, the Third World countries need additional land for agriculture, and they need the foreign currency from the sale of their timber to pay the interest to the rich nations on their debts. Not unreasonably, the Third World countries are suggesting that if the developed countries want them to stop cutting down the rain forests, then they must pay for it.

Other environmental problems include using up the world's resources – such as minerals and fossil fuels. Again, the rich nations are mainly the culprits, but the Third World nations aspire to the standard of living currently enjoyed by the richer nations and this will exacerbate the problem.

In the UK approximately 61 per cent of the emissions which cause global warming come from carbon dioxide, and three-quarters of this figure is emitted by power stations, industry and road transport. Nearly all businesses could do more to reduce their use of power, road fuel and water. It will perhaps be necessary for the government to provide greater incentives, as has been the case with unleaded petrol.

However, much more could be done by individuals and those in positions of authority at all levels.

> **THINK POINT**
>
> What steps do you take at present, at work, to help the environment, and what further steps could you take?

SUMMARY

Whilst much of this chapter is provided to give a basic framework on which to build further knowledge, the environmental issues directly affect the role of the supervisor/first line manager. The careful use of resources to avoid wastage of power, fossil fuels, minerals, paper, water etc., and the control of pollution, are all part of that role.

Supervisory Management Standards:

Unit 2 Contribute to the planning, monitoring and control of resources
Element 2.1 Plan the use of resources
Element 2.2 Monitor and control the use of resources

In this chapter we have looked at:

- markets and competition

  the conditions required in a perfect market
  monopolies
  oligopolies
  governmental intervention in markets
  the effects of marketing and advertising on markets

- factors of production

  land
  labour and population
  capital, including joint ventures, in the Third World

- government

  local government
  central government
  the role of government in the economy
  the European Community

    the European Parliament
    the European Court of Justice
    the Council of Ministers
    the European Commission

- environmental issues

  global warming
  the ozone layer
  declining resources

FURTHER READING

Alain Anderton, *The Economy in Focus: 1992–3*. CPL, 1992.

John Beardshaw, *Economics – A Student's Guide*, 3rd edn. Pitman, 1992.

J. Beardshaw and David Palfreman, *The Organisation in its Environment*, 4th edn. Pitman, 1990.

F. Stanlake, *Introductory Economics*, 5th edn. Longman, 1989.

Section II

Managing Information

In this section we are going to look at the various aspects of the collection, storage, evaluation and communication of information in a business.

Unit 7 of the Supervisory Management Standards is the one which specifically deals with information, but information is such an integral part of our daily lives, both at home and at work, that it is important in all of the other units as well.

Chapter 8
The Need for Information

Supervisory Management Standards	
Unit 2	Contribute to the planning, monitoring and control of resources
Element 2.2	Monitor and control the use of resources
Unit 7	Provide information and advice for action towards meeting organizational objectives
Element 7.1	Obtain, evaluate, record and store information
Element 7.2	Provide information and advice

Throughout history, leaders have recognized the need for accurate information on which to base decisions. Sometimes this meant information with regard to what their enemies were up to, such as who they were making alliances with, how many men they had, where they were sited etc. This information was necessary to avoid being surprised by an attack. In some countries this is still the case, except that in military matters we now refer to it as 'intelligence'. During the Gulf War accurate intelligence played a vital role in the success of the allies. If the information is not accurate it could be worse than having no information at all, because wrong decisions may be made.

Before the enormous leaps forward in communications in this century, fortunes were made by those who received news from abroad first. For example, bankers and businessmen often employed men, with changes of horses available at strategic places, to be able to get the news of the result of a battle before others. This enabled them to make fortunes on the stock market, as a result of the large changes in prices, when the news was generally available. The case was much the same with news by ship from the Far East or the Americas. These examples are both historic, but we still have needs for information to travel by the fastest and most appropriate means. We can all think of occasions when we have been waiting anxiously for some information, only to find it has been delayed as a result of being posted second class.

We have so far identified two of the key requirements for information – *accuracy* and *timeliness*. Let's consider some of the others.

Information needs to be *relevant*. Sue Wells cannot draw up a balance sheet for the year to 31 March 1993 using the stock figures for the previous year; it must only relate to the year she is dealing with.

We need to have information that is *retrievable* from wherever we have stored it. Sometimes we have someone doing a particular job in our unit, and they make that job their own little empire and do not allow anyone else near it. We know from *Managing People* that this is an example of them needing to feel valued and accepted. It does not help us if they are away and the information we require is inside their brains, or within a personal filing system which no one else can understand. It would be like putting all of the information we require into a strongroom and allowing someone to go on holiday with the key.

Information needs to be *verifiable* or capable of being checked. Is there more than one way of arriving at the same answer? In spy books and films much is made of having other sources of information, so that the decision maker can look at a number of small pieces of intelligence from elsewhere which add up to the same overall picture. Alternatively, can we follow each piece of information back to check its accuracy?

The *format* that the information is in is particularly important nowadays. There is little point in sending information to all of our out-stations throughout the world on computer disc if they do not have the equipment on which to read it.

Finally, information needs to be *complete* and *unambiguous*. It would be very stupid and dangerous to act on a fax which gave us instructions and then finished up by saying 'more pages to follow'. Or a telex from Mombasa which advised us that the consignment from Nairobi is arriving on Monday. Here we would need to know which consignment, as there might be more than one – and where is it arriving? It could be arriving at Mombasa to be shipped, it could be arriving at a port in this country or it could be delivered to our front door. Usually past experience will help us, but this is not always the case and assumptions can be expensive.

So information needs to be:

- Accurate
- Timely
- Relevant
- Retrievable
- Verifiable
- Appropriate format
- Complete and unambiguous

These, then, are the considerations before using information in decision making. If any of these cannot be fulfilled, then we should either be on our guard or be looking for ways of overcoming the problem.

WHY DO WE NEED INFORMATION?

Information in business fulfils a number of purposes. We use it as the basis of our decision making, we communicate to and receive it from others to ensure that we have a common understanding, and we use it as a means of increasing our knowledge.

DATA

Data is the plural form of 'datum'. It means an accepted basis from which inferences or assumptions can be made. Information is frequently based on or extracted from data, and for data to be of use it needs processing in some way. This may be by identifying trends in it, or using it for making calculations, charts, graphs, etc. Before data is processed it is referred to as 'raw data'.

CONFIDENTIALITY

It was Francis Bacon who said that 'information is power': this is as true today as it was when he wrote it at the end of the sixteenth century. Unfortunately it also means that some information of necessity is confidential, but not everyone is able to keep it so. If we think back to Maslow's Hierarchy of Needs in *Managing People*, we will recall that the third level is social. This refers to fitting in and being valued by the others in the group, and one of the ways in which some individuals try to achieve this is by passing on everything that they hear in confidence. This may be connected with work or may be some personal confidence given them by a colleague; and the people they pass the information to may not be at all interested. We can all think of occasions when someone at work has just had to tell us something as long as we did not pass it on, as they had promised that they would keep it a secret. When we become In Charge we need to identify who we can trust with confidential information. The people we like the most – for example, our best friends – may not be amongst them, but should we be passing on the information unless the person concerned needs to know it? The answer here is: probably not. Because we have been promoted we are likely to hear many more pieces of confidential information. The fact that we have been promoted and have been told them indicates that we are trusted, and this would not be the case if we were to try to maintain our social standing with our old colleagues by telling them everything we learn that is confidential.

SOURCES OF INFORMATION

The sources of information at work can be so varied that it is not possible to draw up a definitive list of them here. However, it will help us in considering the subject if we divide it into external information and internal information.

External information is available from government publications, chambers of commerce, trade magazines and various computer data banks. Specialized information can be purchased from outside agencies and consultants and, where necessary, by recruiting specialists.

Internal information comes from all of the records and statistics that we all keep: the number of items produced, sales records, attendance records, overtime, machine faults etc. It also comes from the knowledge, training and experience that the employees have. We receive information from some, we share part of that information or make it available to others who may need it.

If we analyse the use of information in a business, we find that the senior managers who are responsible for the direction that the business or organization takes tend to make the greatest use of external information. They need to know the customer requirements, what the competition are doing, changes in products, changes in the law, the likely movements of the economies both in this country and wherever the company or organization trades or receives supplies from. Obviously they need internal information to ensure that the business is meeting its objectives, but this is much more the province of the middle managers.

The middle managers are likely to receive information from both internal and external sources, as they are the people who run the business on a medium-term basis. A large part of their function is planning, which is, of course, in the future. Front line managers/ supervisors make the greatest use of internal information, as their responsibilities are for the day-to-day running of the business. While a large part of the middle manager's job is planning, for the first line manager/supervisor it tends to be organizing.

Planning is always for the future, organizing is in the present.

Management Level	*Decisions Timescale*	*Sources of Information*
Senior	Long Months and years	Largely external
Middle	Medium Weeks and months	Internal and external
First	Short Hours and days	Mainly internal

THINK POINT

Draw a diagram showing all of the places from which you receive information, who you share it with or make it available to, and to whom you provide information.

INFORMATION OVERLOAD

There is very definitely a limit to how much information each of us can absorb and process at any one time, and attempts to exceed this can lead to a breakdown in health.

Whilst the last statement was written with people in mind, it can be applied equally to businesses and organizations. Within the work environment there is now too much information which causes problems in terms of the time spent in collecting, processing and distributing it. In the days when copies were produced by using carbon paper, the number of people within an organization who received a copy of a report, letter, memo etc. was very limited. Nowadays there is a tendency for the author of a report or letter to feel that it is of interest to a far greater number of people, or that certain people might feel slighted if they are not kept informed. Consequently it is photocopied or printed in far greater numbers than in the carbon paper days; or communicated by electronic mail. It must then be read, or at least scanned, by the recipients to ensure that they do not overlook something of real importance. Because of the increasing volumes of information important items are often overlooked, misfiled or not diarized for action. From an organizational point of view, so much information is sometimes collected and stored that the organization is unable to make use of it for decision-making purposes. It would take far too long to process it into the form required, and the decision might be an urgent one.

INFORMATION DISTORTION

Information may be distorted, manipulated or simply withheld at times when employees of whatever status have something they wish to cover up. This can apply to all sorts of mistakes or examples of poor performance, or the desire to be seen to be better than they are. In this context, information can be withheld, sieved or exaggerated. In our daily work, when a subordinate reports on how a job is going or why something is late, it may be worthwhile to wonder what we are not being told and how much is being exaggerated. Other examples of information distortion occur when someone is trying to put across a particular point of view. No salesman or saleswoman ever tells you the faults of the goods you are proposing to purchase, and even if you ask on a specific point of weakness the answer is unlikely to put you off from buying. When we look at making presentations we shall be looking at ways of presenting information which gain the acceptance of the majority of the audience. The danger with this, from the audience's point of view, lies in how much they are not being told and what information is being exaggerated. At the beginning of this chapter we said that information needed to be verifiable, that is, capable of being checked, preferably from another source.

SUMMARY

Supervisory Management Standards:

Unit 2	Contribute to the planning, monitoring and control of resources
Element 2.2	Monitor and control the use of resources
Unit 7	Provide information and advice for action towards meeting organizational objectives
Element 7.1	Obtain, evaluate, record and store information
Element 7.2	Provide information and advice

In this chapter we have looked at why we need information, and have identified that it should be:

Accurate
Timely
Relevant
Easily retrievable
Verifiable
In the appropriate format
Complete and unambiguous

- We have considered the meaning of data and raw data, and how they are used to provide information.
- We discussed the need for confidentiality, and the need to decide who should be trusted with information.
- We looked at the sources of information and how they are likely to differ according to the level of seniority of the work.
- The problems of information overload were examined.
- We looked at the need to be aware of the possible misuse of information through distortion, manipulation and withholding.

Chapter 9

Using Numbers

Supervisory Management Standards	
Unit 2	Contribute to the planning, monitoring and control of resources
Element 2.1	Plan the use of resources
Element 2.2	Monitor and control the use of resources
Unit 7	Provide information and advice for action towards meeting organizational objectives
Element 7.1	Obtain, evaluate, record and store information
Element 7.2	Provide information and advice

It is often the way in which raw data is laid out that enables information to be drawn from it. In this chapter we shall be looking at the various main formats that can be used. In these days of aiming for total quality and user friendliness, charts, tables and graphs etc. should be instantly understood. It can be extremely frustrating trying to understand a bus or railway timetable, or accommodation guide, which uses codes, asterisks, etc. the key to which is difficult to find. Many holiday brochures are poorly laid out for finding the exact details of a holiday in terms of price or meals included. We shall be examining some basic rules to assist us in laying out data in charts and graphs, but first let us set up a typical example of a poor layout and see how we can improve it.

Case Note 6

John is the senior clerk in the Accounts and Finance Department at the head office of Topicflex Ltd, the packaging manufacturing company. He has been requested by the company accountant to extract information on the telephone bills for four of the head office departments for the last three years. So that he could be certain of providing the right amount of information and in the most suitable format, John asked the accountant the reason for the request and who the information was intended for. The accountant explained that he believed that the bills were getting progressively higher, and that the sales people were using the telephone too much and might even be making personal calls.

The following is the data that John extracted:

Phone calls

Accounts	199X	12
	199Y	13
	199Z	15
Personnel	199X	14
	199Y	15
	199Z	16
Admin	199X	6
	199Y	7
	199Z	9
Sales	199X	43
	199Y	45
	199Z	46

If John gives the data to the accountant in this form, will he or she have to waste time in altering it to look more meaningful?

One of the things that the accountant was looking for was a comparison of the figures, and as the figures for each department for the different years are next to one another this can be easily seen. However, it does not really show by how much the telephone bills have increased overall, so anyone using it would need to calculate this for themselves. Furthermore, if the accountant wants to pass a copy to another senior manager, for example the sales manager, it will be necessary to add some better headings so that it can be understood immediately. Some additional columns showing percentage increases over the previous year would also help. A better layout is shown in exhibit 9.1.

We can now see that the telephone costs overall for the last year have risen 7.5% as against the previous one, which was 6.7% higher than the year before that. The main heading explains exactly what the purpose of the chart is and states the units of measurement that have been used. The notes underneath the chart state who extracted the

Exhibit 9.1 Topicflex Ltd head office, annual telephone costs in £000s

Department	199X	199Y	% increase on last year	199Z	% increase on last year
Accounts & Fin.	12	13	8.3	15	15.4
Personnel	14	15	7.1	16	6.7
Administration	6	7	16.7	9	28.6
Sales	43	45	4.7	46	2.2
Totals	75	80	6.7	86	7.5

Notes

Compiled by John Anderson, 21 January 199A.
Source: Departmental budget actuals, years 199X, 199Y and 199Z. All figures rounded to the nearest thousand pounds.

information, when and where from. They also make it clear how the figures have been rounded to the nearest thousand pounds. Because in this second example John has borne in mind the accountant's reasons for requesting the data, he has set it out so that the information is immediately obvious. What now stands out is that it is not the sales department that has been using the telephone more, but the accountant's own department and the administration department. It will now be necessary for someone to find out the reasons for the increases: they will have to analyse the figures in greater depth, without rounding them up as John has done. The main thing is that they will know, without having to consult him, exactly how and where he obtained his data.

The two examples clearly show how, by setting out data in a more meaningful way, the communication of statistical information can become far more effective. Also, by finding out exactly why the information is required and by whom, it is possible to get it right the first time and so save time and money.

Before starting to draw up a chart or table it is necessary to identify in your mind or enquire who it is for, why they want it and what they will be looking for. Or, if you are providing it because you want something as a result, ask yourself what conclusions you want the readers to be able to draw from it.

The guidelines to bear in mind when constructing or looking at charts and tables are:

1. They should have a title or heading which clearly indicates the purpose and content.
2. Enough space should be allowed so that the layout is clear and uncluttered.
3. Each row and column should have a heading which, whilst short, is self-explanatory.
4. Care should be taken to avoid the use of abbreviations in row and column headings unless they are really obvious.
5. The units of measurement should be shown.
6. Where sets of data are being compared, they should be sited close to one another.
7. Where statistics have been calculated from the data, such as percentages, they should be sited next to the figures they relate to.
8. Any omissions from the data should be explained in the notes.
9. Any treatment of the numbers, such as rounding up or down, should be explained in the notes.
10. The source of the data and the date extracted should be shown in the notes.
11. The name or reference of the person who compiled the chart or table should be shown.

THINK POINT

When you last drew up a chart would the person for whom it was intended have had to make further calculations to find the information he or she needed?

If the accountant had spoken to the sales manager about his suspicions before getting John to extract the data he might have received short shrift. Sales departments are always looking for trends developing in their markets and product sales figures as a means of identifying where each product is in its life cycle, where the opportunities are, etc. In this particular company the sales manager liked to monitor his departmental costs in a similar way, and would therefore have been able to refute any suggestion of excessive telephone usage.

In the sales department of Topicflex Ltd, Penny, who was the sales administrator, had set up a monitoring system at the request of her boss, the sales manager. She entered the departmental bills into the computer as they were received and authorized, and at the end of each quarter she could obtain printouts in graph form for the total expenditure, groups of expenditure and specific items like the telephone bill. The budgeted figures were shown as a separate line on the graph, so it was possible to see at a glance how close to budget the department was working.

So far we have looked at data displayed in tabular form to yield its information. We are now going to look at a number of alternative formats which can illustrate data more effectively.

1 Graphs
2 Bar charts
3 Gantt charts
4 Pie charts
5 Histograms
6 Pictograms

GRAPHS

Graphs are drawn to illustrate the relationship between two variables. When properly used and constructed they provide an immediate idea of the way the relationship is moving. As that makes it sound like some sort of bug or monitoring device on a first date, let us start to construct a graph in stages.

First of all we need to look at the data relating to the two variables, and for this example we have chosen to use the monthly cash receipts figures taken from the cash flow forecast of Wells (Plumbers) Ltd in the budgeting chapter. That may only sound like one variable, but the other is made up by the time factor in months:

Apl	May	June	Jly	Aug	Sep
12.0	11.5	12.25	11.5	9.5	10.75
Oct	Nov	Dec	Jan	Feb	Mar
11.5	13.5	14.0	14.5	14.25	14.0

As we can see, the range of the figures is from 9.5 to 14.5, which is not very large. Unfortunately this means that we shall have a large amount of wasted space if we start from zero. We draw two lines, one vertical and one horizontal, which touch. These are called the vertical axis and the horizontal axis. Periods of time are nearly always entered on the horizontal axis. To do this we simply divide the line up with a ruler to fit in the number of minutes, hours, days, weeks, months etc. that we require. Similarly, the vertical axis is ruled up to accommodate the range of figures we need to enter. We then plot the figures one by one onto the graph. The first one is entered above the April marker at the level for its value of 12.0. When all the figures have been plotted they are joined by a smooth curving line. We can see the results of this in figure 9.1.

As we can see, the graph has taken up most of the page and the line itself is stuck in the top third of it. Obviously this could have been much worse, as the figures could have been in the range 109.5 to 114.5 or even more. The rules for drawing graphs demand that the numbering of the vertical axis, wherever practical, should start at zero. Where it is not practical for this to be done, it should be made very

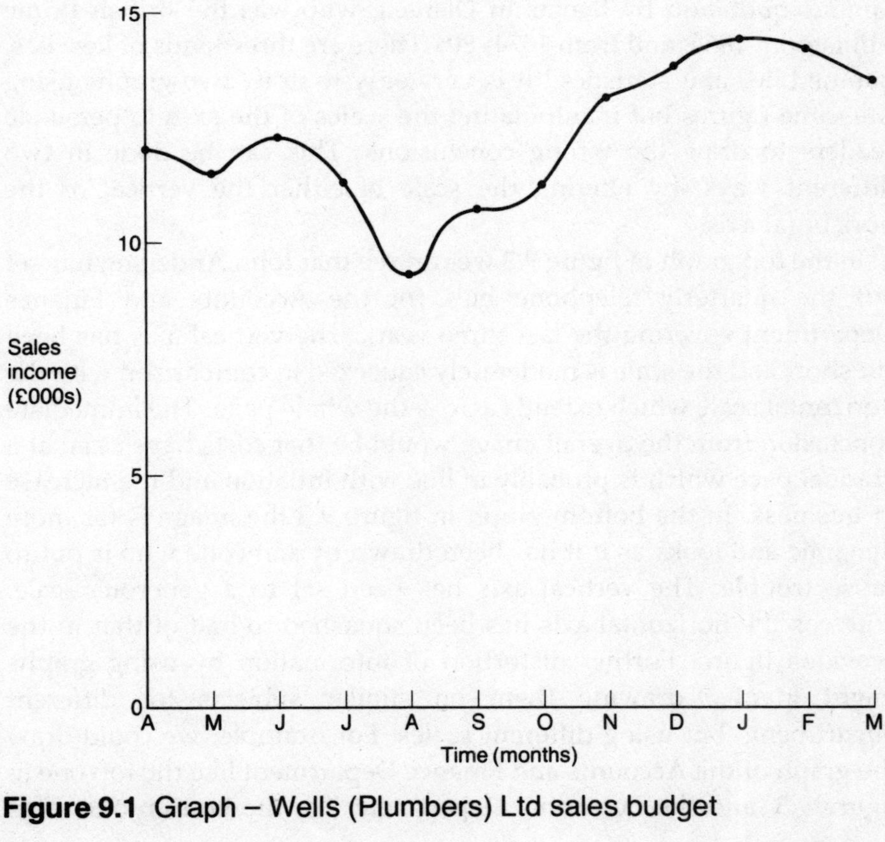

Figure 9.1 Graph – Wells (Plumbers) Ltd sales budget

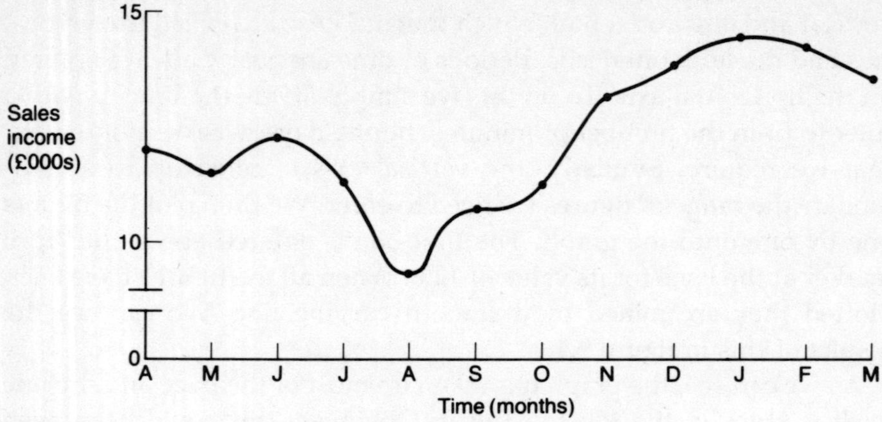

Figure 9.2 Modified version of figure 9.1

clear by entering a zero at the start and then breaking the line in some way to show that the scale is not continuous, as in figure 9.2.

The reason for this apparent ritual can, in a sense, be found in the famous quotation by Benjamin Disraeli, who was the British Prime Minister in 1868, and from 1874–80: 'There are three kinds of lies: lies, damned lies and statistics.' It is very easy to draw two graphs using the same figures but manipulating the scales of the axes to persuade readers to draw the wrong conclusions. This can be done in two different ways: by altering the scale of either the vertical or the horizontal axis.

In the top graph in figure 9.3 we can see that John Anderson has set out the quarterly telephone bills for the Accounts and Finance Department covering the last three years. The vertical axis has been cut short and the scale is moderately squeezed in comparison with the horizontal scale which extends across the whole page. The immediate conclusion from the overall image would be that costs have risen at a gradual pace which is probably in line with inflation and the increase in business. In the bottom graph in figure 9.3 the image is far more dynamic and looks as if it has been drawn by someone who is out to cause trouble. The vertical axis has been set to a generous scale, whereas the horizontal axis has been squashed to half of that in the previous figure. Further distortion of information by using graphs might involve drawing them on similar subjects for different departments but using different scales. For example, we could draw the graph of the Accounts and Finance Department like the top one in figure 9.3, and the Personnel Department like the bottom one. This

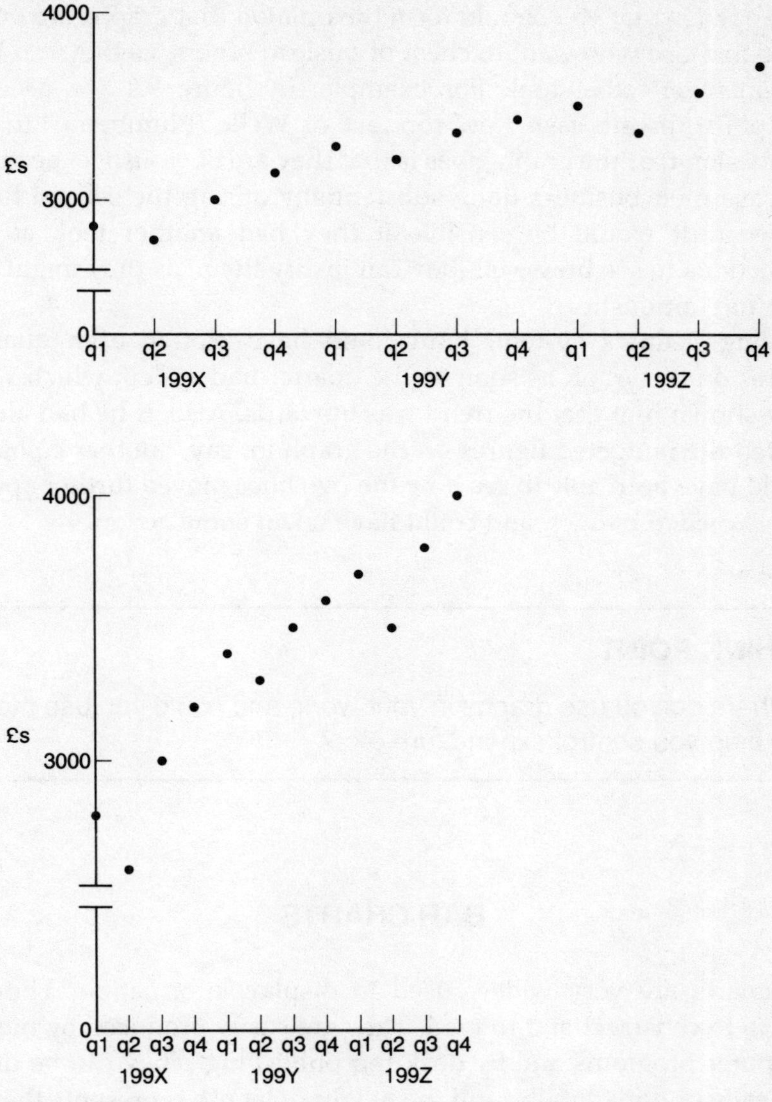

Figure 9.3 Two different graphic interpretations of the Accounts and Finance Dept telephone bills

would give the (totally wrong) impression that the telephone increases in Accounts were less than those in Personnel. Another distortion can be caused by omitting to show that the graph did not start at zero, and starting the one it is being compared with at zero.

We have emphasized the need to be careful with the construction of graphs so that they do not mislead, and that you must be vigilant and not misled by those presented to you by others. What we do not want to happen is that you should form the opinion that graphs are only of value to those who want to cheat or mislead others, as they can be an extremely effective tool. For example, in figure 9.1 we used the receipts from the cash flow forecast of Wells (Plumbers) Ltd. The impression that the graph gives is that they are obviously expecting to increase their business quite substantially during the second half of the year. It would be sensible if they had another look at their predictions to see how well they can justify them, as they might have been too optimistic.

Using Penny's system, John could have plotted each quarter's figures on his graph as soon as the quarter had ended, which would have shown him that the trend was upwards. Also, if he had already plotted the budgeted figures on the graph in, say, another colour, he would have been able to see how the two lines moved further apart as bills exceeded budget, and could have taken some action.

THINK POINT

Where do you use graphs in your work, and could you use more to help you control expenditure etc.?

BAR CHARTS

Bar charts are very widely used to display information. They are simple to construct and to read. They are easily produced by modern computer programs and by desk-top publishing. They can be drawn vertically or horizontally, and the height or length represents the level of the data. The bars are usually drawn of the same width on any one chart. The examples in figure 9.4 demonstrate how the same information can be displayed either horizontally or vertically. Use has been made of the horizontal format to add more explanation.

Simple trends can be seen from bar charts, but they do not have the same facility to be able to project a trend in the same way that graphs do.

There are a number of variations on the simple bar charts shown in figure 9.4. For example, if we needed to show how the figures for the

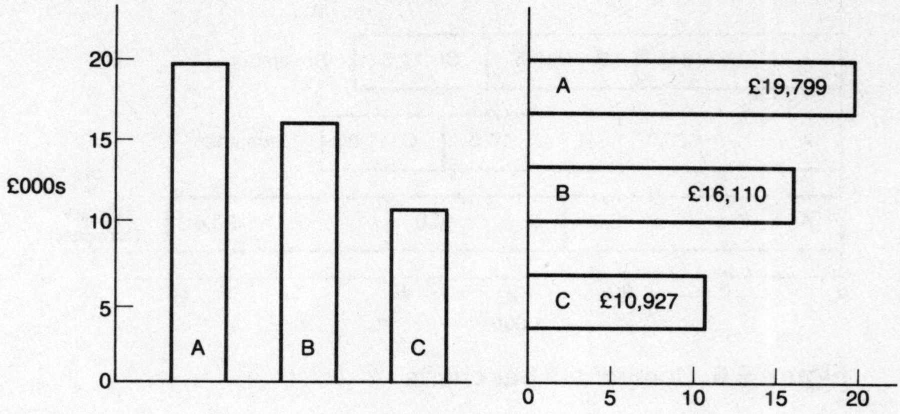

Figure 9.4 Vertical and horizontal bar charts

sales areas in figure 9.4 compared as against the previous month and the forecast for the following month, we could have a chart like the one in figure 9.5.

This particular variation is referred to as a 'compound bar chart'. Figure 9.6 shows the information from figure 9.5 drawn as a 'component bar chart'. This emphasizes, in this case, the size of the problem in reaching the January forecast.

It is interesting to note how these last two charts have used the same information, and yet each has highlighted certain problems rather better than the other. The compound bar chart (figure 9.5) highlights the problem with sales area C and, to a lesser extent, area A; whereas the component bar chart (figure 9.6) highlights the overall picture by showing that the three areas are jointly far below the January forecast level.

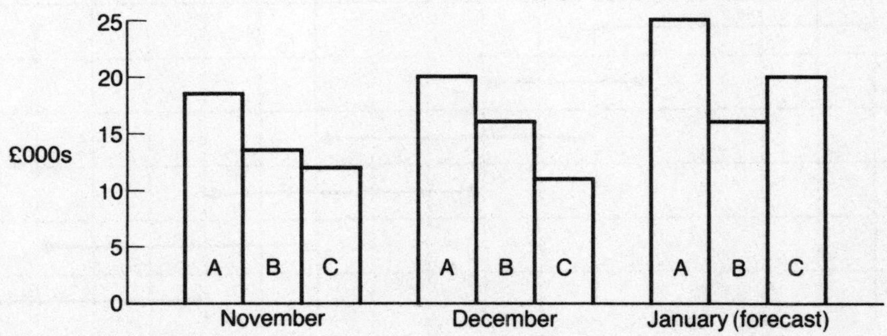

Figure 9.5 Compound bar charts

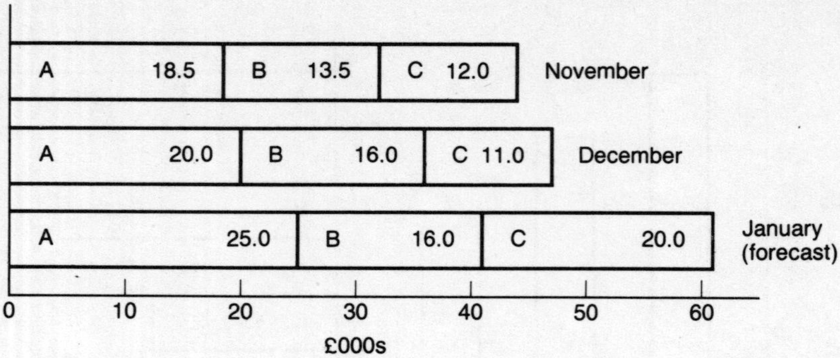

Figure 9.6 Component bar charts

GANTT CHARTS

Gantt charts are named after Henry Gantt, who worked at Bethlehem Steel under F. W. Taylor (who we met in *Managing People*). They are horizontal bar charts which show the progress of activities across a span of time (see figure 9.7). The horizontal axis is always used for the time and the vertical axis for the various activities. They are widely used in a variety of forms for planning work, and are discussed in *In Charge, Managing Operations*.

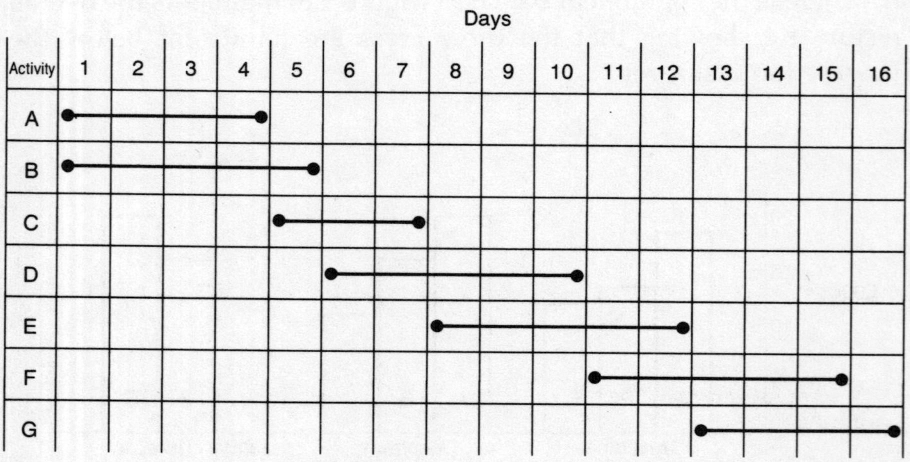

Figure 9.7 A Gantt chart

> **THINK POINT**
>
> What Gantt charts are used at your place of work?

PIE CHARTS

These are circular charts where the circle represents the total quantity of a variable, such as the total expenditure by a district council. The circle is then divided into segments which are proportionate to the values of the components of the variable. For example, if housing represents, say, 42 per cent of the district council's expenditure, then there should be a segment that is 42 per cent of the circle for housing – a large slice of the pie! They are easy to produce on computer, but would be very complicated to calculate and produce manually if one wanted to be accurate. They therefore tend to be used to represent the approximate proportions of the values only (see figure 9.8).

What can we learn from pie charts? For overall comparative purposes, not very much. The pie for January is obviously larger than the others, but the one for December is so slightly larger than the one for November that the difference could easily be overlooked. The proportions of the segments for November and December appear to be the same, but in January C has expanded at the expense of B. We know from the figures we have used (see figure 9.6) that those for sales area B are the same in the pie for December as in January, but we would be unable to judge this purely from the two pie charts. It is difficult to estimate the areas of non-rectangular shapes.

We will look at one more example of a pie chart and then draw up some simple rules based on our findings. The chart in figure 9.9 is typical of the use to which pie charts are put.

Figure 9.9 has a very clear message with regard to the size of the staff costs in relation to the other costs, and draws attention to the smallest segment, sales and advertising, by starting to remove that piece of the pie. The fact that there are no material costs involved leads us to the assumption that this relates to a service industry such as a travel agent. The chart would probably be used as part of the annual report to staff on the year's performance, or perhaps as part of the argument as to why a smaller than requested pay offer should be

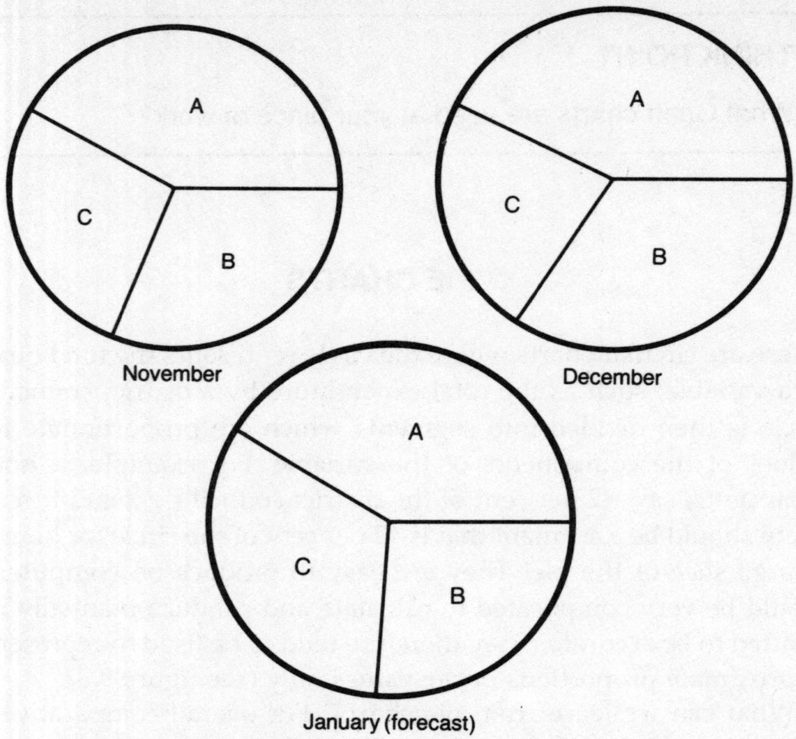

Figure 9.8 Pie charts

accepted. The segments would probably be printed in different colours, as technology has moved very rapidly in this area. The desktop publishing facilities in even quite small companies and organizations are now capable of a very professional quality of colour printing.

So far we have suggested that the areas of the segments should be proportional to the quantity of the variable they relate to. For example, in figure 9.9, as the staff costs are 67 per cent of the total costs, the segment takes up 67 per cent of the circle. In practice, however, this is not always followed, as the pie is used more to illustrate the proportional relationship between, say, the staff costs and the other costs. The segments may therefore only be approximate.

The conclusions we can draw from these examples are:

1 Pie charts can be used to illustrate where there has been a large increase by using pies of different sizes.
2 They can be used to illustrate a major category.

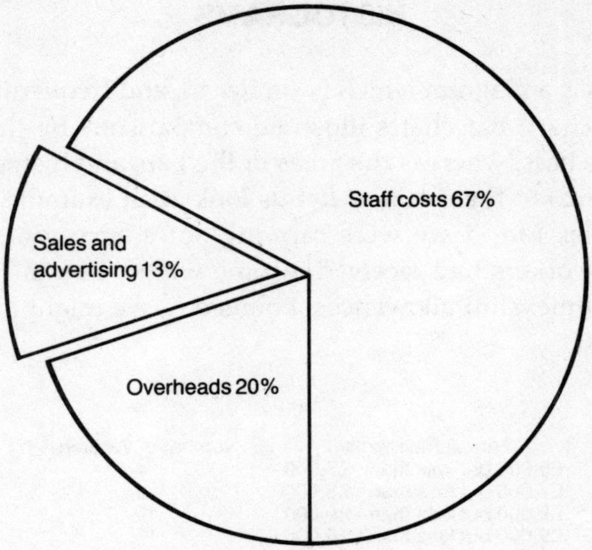

Figure 9.9 Pie chart – segment removed

3 They can draw attention to a small category by making the segment stand away from the pie.
4 They do not demonstrate the exact amount of any change.
5 Segments often appear the same size even though the statistics are different.
6 In the case where comparisons are being drawn between two or more pies, if there is a smaller segment of a larger pie, it is not possible to identify which way the value has changed, if at all. In figure 9.8, in the pie charts for December and January, the value of segment B is the same, but this is not obvious.
7 The segments are not always easy to write on.
8 The number of segments needs to be limited to no more than six.

THINK POINT

Which information in your job would you present to others in bar chart form, and which in pie chart form?

HISTOGRAMS

A histogram is a diagram which is similar to, and frequently confused with, a bar chart. Bar charts illustrate comparisons by the height or length of the bars, whereas the areas of the bars and histograms must be proportional to their values. Let us look at an example.

At Topicflex Ltd, if we were carrying out a survey of how many production workers had received income within certain ranges from wages, overtime, shift allowances, bonus etc., we might find the data in figure 9.10.

Annual Payments	Number of Workers
£5,000 but less than £7,000	4
£7,000 but less than £8,000	6
£8,000 but less than £9,000	12
£9,000 but less than £10,000	16
£10,000 but less than £11,000	20
£11,000 but less than £12,000	16
£12,000 but less than £13,000	10
£13,000 but less than £15,000	6

Note that the first and last lines cover a range of £2,000

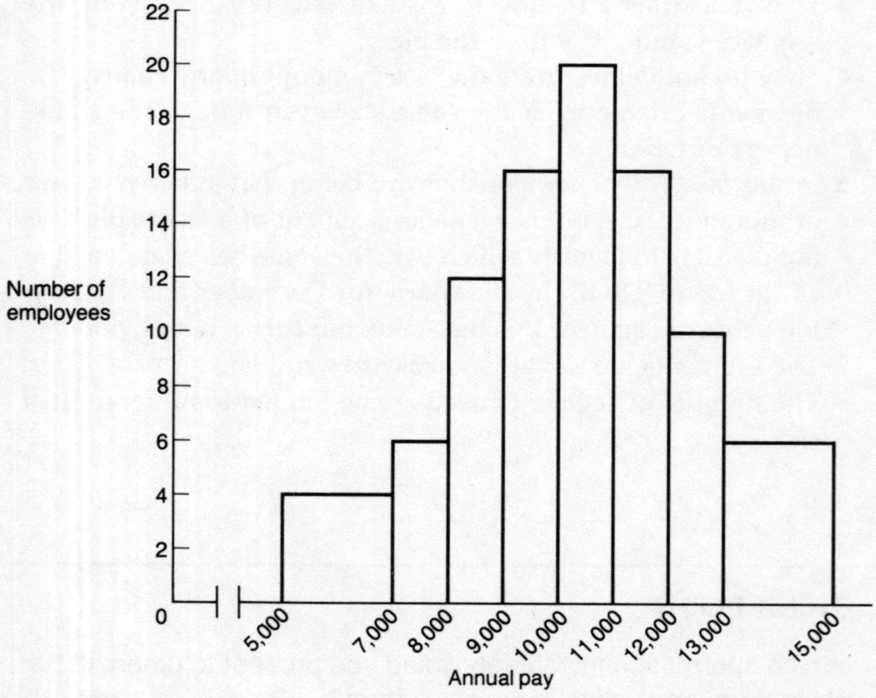

Figure 9.10 Histogram

In figure 9.10 we can see that the bars indicate the number of employees between certain levels of income. Also, care has been taken to make the first and last blocks reflect the fact that they each cover double the range of payments of the remaining blocks. This is essential with histograms. Histogram blocks do not have spaces between them, and do not have any description on them. Each bar must show the same thing, so that the scale of the bottom axis is a continuous measure of the same thing. In bar charts we could show different products or sales areas in bars that are next to one another, but with a space in between for greater emphasis.

PICTOGRAMS

A pictogram is not a funny birthday greeting, like a kissagram, it is a 'picture diagram' where pictures are used to represent the data. They provide a strong visual impact, but the data has to be simple. They can be drawn in different ways, and it will probably help if we have a look at some examples.

In figure 9.11 we can see how the size of two different removal firms has been illustrated by use of a pictogram. Obviously it is not possible to demonstrate the difference in size with any accuracy, so the statistics written on the pictogram help to overcome this. In the second pictogram, figure 9.12, pin men have been used to indicate the reduction in the workforce from 1980 to 1990, with one pin man equalling one thousand workers. Again the message is immediately obvious, but parts of pin men are not very accurate, and the key is a necessary feature. Many pictograms can be difficult to draw.

The main feature of the pictogram is that it has a strong, visual image which could be a lasting one. However, it has to use simple data, preferably in whole units. More complex data is better expressed by a bar chart.

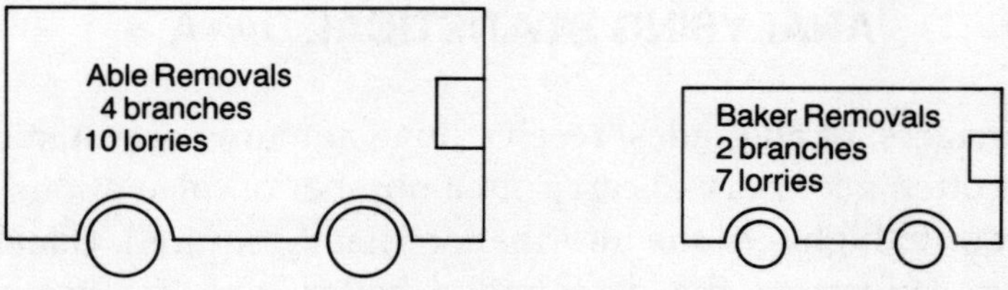

Figure 9.11 Pictogram – removal vans

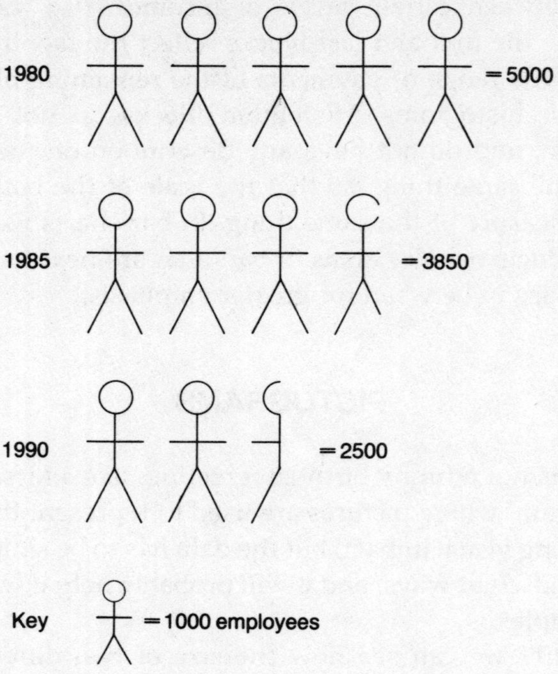

Figure 9.12 Pictogram – pin men

> **THINK POINT**
>
> What examples of the use of pictograms can you think of in your workplace?

ANALYSING STATISTICAL DATA

Most managers, of all grades, receive huge amounts of statistical raw data. It is often necessary to carry out a number of calculations with it to extract or to highlight the information that is required. Usually this will mean converting the data into a better form for comparison purposes, and there are several ways of doing this.

Percentages

When John presented the data regarding the telephone bills to the accountant he added two columns which showed the percentage increases. Calculating percentages is one way of analysing statistical data.

'Per cent' means per hundred, so thirty per cent means thirty per hundred items, pounds or whatever is being calculated. Even the familiar per cent sign (%) is made up of a one and two zeros. If we look again at John's table (in exhibit 9.2), we can see how effective the calculation is in bringing the figures for the four departments into a common form which makes comparison that much easier.

For most people, the quickest and easiest way to calculate percentages is by using a pocket or desk calculator. For example, if we want to calculate 17½% of £243 we would simply enter 243 × 17.5%. This is very easy as long as we remember that in mathematics 'of' means 'multiply'. If we want to add 20% to 456 we would enter 456 + 20% and, similarly, to deduct 20% it would be 456 − 20%. If you do not have a calculator or computer available, or choose not to use one, the manual calculations would be as follows.

To calculate 17½% of 243 the equation we need is

$$\frac{17.5 \times 100}{243} = \frac{1750}{243}$$

It would then be necessary to carry out a long division calculation of 1750 divided by 243.

Exhibit 9.2 Topicflex Ltd head office, annual telephone costs in £000s

Department	199X	199Y	% increase on last year	199Z	% increase on last year
Accounts & Fin.	12	13	8.3	15	15.4
Personnel	14	15	7.1	16	6.7
Administration	6	7	16.7	9	28.6
Sales	43	45	4.7	46	2.2
Totals	75	80	6.7	86	7.5

2 The mean, the median and the mode

The *mean*, or arithmetic mean, to give it its more accurate title, is the average to which most of us refer when we think we are talking about averages. That sounds like a piece of gobbledegook so let's look at some examples. The *mean* is calculated by adding all of the values of the items together and then dividing the answer by the number of items. If asked to calculate the average, that is how nearly all of us would have gone about it. The mean has the advantage of being an accurate arithmetic calculation and can therefore be used when this is important.

Unfortunately, we also talk about the average price of things when we mean the price that occurs the most frequently. For example, we might say that the average price of a cup of coffee when bought out is 50 pence, if that is the price that we are charged the most often. Here what we are referring to is not the arithmetic mean but the *mode*, which is the price which is charged the most often. The mode is a very convenient way of referring to the 'usual size' or 'normal price' of items.

The *median* is the middle number of a set of numbers which have been placed in order. If there are eleven numbers which have been arranged in ascending or descending order, then the sixth one would be the median. If there are an even number of items, the middle two are added together and divided by two to find the median. The median has the advantage of removing distortions that can affect the mean sometimes, such as where there are a few very high or very low (untypical) values in a set.

Let us have a look at an example of a row of numbers and calculate the mean, median and mode from it. We will stay with the prices of cups of coffee:

30p 35p 40p 40p 45p 45p 45p 50p 50p 50p 50p 65p 70p = £6.15

If we divide the total by the number of values we would be dividing £6.15 by 13, which comes to 47.3p, so the *mean* is 47.3p. The middle number out of the set of thirteen has to be the seventh one, so the *median* is 45p. The value which occurs the most frequently is 50p, as it occurs four times, so the *mode* is 50p.

3 Ratios

A ratio expresses the relationship between two amounts to enable comparisons to be drawn from them. The results are expressed either as fractions or, more normally, in the format x:y (said as 'x to y'). Sometimes, as in chapter 5, results may be expressed as percentages or so many days or weeks.

In John's figures for the telephone bills for 199Z he had Accounts and Finance Department with a total for the year of £15,000, and the Administration Department with a total of £9,000. In this case we would say that telephone costs between the two departments were in a ratio of 5:3 (five to three). This has been calculated by reducing the figures by dividing each by the highest number that both are divisible by, which, in this case, is 3,000.

Calculators

We have mentioned the use of calculators in this chapter, and it would be wrong to leave the subject without adding a word of caution with regard to their use. In the last chapter we mentioned that information needs to be verifiable and that some means of checking its accuracy is necessary. Most calculators do not have a paper tally roll, so there is not an audit trail available. Because of the ease with which we can wrongly key an entry without noticing, it is necessary to check our answers each time we use a calculator. A check to ensure that the answer is approximately correct is usually sufficient.

SUMMARY

Supervisory Management Standards:

Unit 2 Contribute to the planning, monitoring and control of resources
Element 2.1 Plan the use of resources
Element 2.2 Monitor and control the use of resources

Unit 7 Provide information and advice for action towards meeting organizational objectives
Element 7.1 Obtain, evaluate, record and store information
Element 7.2 Provide information and advice

In this chapter we have looked at how to set out data in charts so that the information is obvious. We have drawn up some rules to assist us.

We have looked at how to draw graphs and how to avoid distortions in the way they present the data.

We have also seen examples of bar charts, Gantt charts, pie charts, histograms and pictograms, and examined the advantages and disadvantages of each as a means of presenting information.

In analysing statistical data we looked at percentages, mean, median, mode and ratios, how they are calculated and what they mean.

Finally, we discussed the use of calculators and how we need to check the answers.

FURTHER READING

Tim Hannagan, *The Effective Use of Statistics*. Kogan Page, 1990.

Chapter 10

Storing and Retrieving Information

Supervisory Management Standards	
Unit 7	Provide information and advice for action towards meeting organizational objectives
Element 7.1	Obtain, evaluate, record and store information
Element 7.2	Provide information and advice

In this chapter we are going to look at various ways of storing information. In each case we shall examine how effectively the information can be accessed or recalled from that particular type of storage. In chapter 8, when we listed the main characteristics that we considered to be essential for good information, one of the first was that it should be retrievable.

MEMORY

Our own memory is probably the storage system that we use the most. It is run by that incredibly powerful computer that each of us has inside our heads which has a phenomenal capacity. Unfortunately, as we grow older our ability to recall information can decline. This can be largely explained by the fact that the longer we live the more information and experiences we have stored.

Our memory stores information in pictures, sounds, smells, tastes and textures. If we are asked to describe the way to somewhere in town we will visualize the route at the same time as we describe it. If we are asked to describe the Eiffel Tower in Paris we will find the picture in our memory and then start to describe it from the picture. If we are asked what something tastes like we will describe it in terms of other tastes that we recall. If we hear a piece of music that sounds familiar we can usually recall what it is or where we have heard it before. Often these senses are linked, and when, for example, we hear a piece of music, we can recall the scene of where we were when we last heard it. Those of us who are old enough can recall where we were and what we were doing when we heard that President Kennedy had been assassinated. Sometimes it is a smell that reminds us of something that we have not thought of for many years. For example, the smell of the malt as we pass a brewery may bring back memories of junior school if that was situated near to a brewery.

All too often we rely solely on our memories when really we ought to make some record to back it up. We have all probably had the experience in our school days or whilst on courses of not taking notes, or of taking insufficient notes, because the subject matter appeared obvious or was just 'common sense'. Then later in an examination, or when we needed to use the information, it was no longer obvious or just 'common sense', and some form of back-up notes would have been welcome.

The main problem with relying on our memories for information storage are access and retrievability. We have already discussed some problems we might have with retrieving information we have stored in our memories, but the biggest problem is that others can only access that information through us, unless it is known to others or is recorded elsewhere. If the sole store of information is our memory, that can indeed be power, providing others know that we have the information. However, if we think of the example we looked at in chapter 7, if we are not available it is like locking all of the information in a strong room and sending someone on holiday with the only key. The other main problem with using our memory as the only storage relates to the type of information. We are less likely to use memory as the sole store of something which, at the time, we consider to be reasonably complex. This links back to what we were saying earlier about not making notes where the subject appeared to be obvious or simply common sense.

The major advantages of using our memory include the speed of recall for information we use the most, the huge capacity for some types of data, such as foreign vocabulary, and the complete confidentiality.

GIGO

GIGO is an acronym for 'garbage in, garbage out', meaning that the quality of the information retrieved from storage depends on the quality of what was put in originally. This expression is usually used in relation to computer storage, but it applies equally to our memory storage of information (we have already likened the brain to a huge computer). If we take in bad information and believe it, it will distort our judgement in all decisions relating to that subject thereafter. It is likely that we all took in a certain amount of 'garbage' during our formative period at 3–6 years of age, which will influence the ways we think and react to certain things even now.

Changing the information that we hold from 'garbage' is often quite difficult. If we are introduced to a number of people and for some reason mix up the names of two of them, so that in our minds we record that Mr A is Mr B and vice versa, it will be quite hard for us to correct this unless we see them daily. Whilst we shall no longer be certain that Mr A is Mr B, we are likely to be unsure which one is which for some time.

It is usually believed that when we are listening to others our concentration is such that, at best, we only hear two-thirds of what is being said and take in even less. This in itself can be a cause of GIGO, and we shall look at this in greater detail in the next chapter, when we consider providing and presenting information.

PERSONAL ORGANIZER SYSTEM

The now familiar leather personal organizer which is carried by many managers is, unfortunately, not used as widely as it should be. This is probably a result of the cost both of the initial system and the replacement pages, as well as because it is a new way of working and forces new habits to be adopted. Many people still believe that it is simply an overgrown and somewhat 'posey' diary, but this is far from the truth.

In *Managing People* we discussed the fact that one of the main roles of a manager is planning. A personal organizer should contain your key result areas and goals plus the plans you have made for achieving them. Information relating to the plans and other information you require – such as names, telephone numbers, addresses, technical information – should also be held within them. If you also use the system as your diary, then everything is together in one place which, together with your memory, enables you to be effective even when you are away from your place of work.

Case Note 7

Karen Wells, who is In Charge of the domestic plumbing work of Wells (Plumbers) Ltd, spends most of her time away from their base. So far, the company has not invested in mobile telephones, on the basis of expense, so Karen telephones the office once a day, at lunch time, to pick up any messages. Because she is away from the office so much, Karen started to operate a personal organizer system. She keeps this with her all of the time, and now that she has got used to it she is far more organized and could not work without it. She uses it for all of her personal business as well, such as keeping a record of her personal budget, insurance details etc.

She uses a sort of Gantt chart to schedule each major job, such as central heating installations. This shows her the name, address and telephone number of the customer, when the work was promised for, when the parts were ordered and the promised delivery date, when any associated building work is to be carried out, how long the job is scheduled to take. The dates are carried forward into her diary section, so that she can see what she should be doing each day and when she should be chasing the parts up. She gives a copy of her weekly schedule and the Gantt charts to Sue, so that she is in a position to respond to any customer or supplier queries and to book additional work for Karen when she is available. Karen also keeps some technical information on new boilers and control systems in her organizer, until she is familiar with them. This she does by reducing the manufacturer's information sheets on the photocopier to the same size as her personal organizer system, punching holes to match those of her organizer and filing it in a separate section for technical information

As a result of Karen's success with her personal organizer system, both Colin and Jack Wells have also started to use them. They both found it difficult at first to remember to enter everything and to discard old habits of relying on memory for when jobs should be done, or when supplies were promised for. However, after one or two embarrassments where things got forgotten and they found that they were double-booked, they soon adopted the new habits necessary to run the system, especially with Sue to remind them!

Instead of buying the forms for their personal organizers pre-printed, Wells (Plumbers) Ltd have designed their own forms, which Sue then photocopies for them.

These systems helped Wells (Plumbers) Ltd to become known for their reliability, which is an essential part of quality and customer care.

MANUAL FILING SYSTEMS

We still receive so much information in paper form that we are unable to read as carefully and to absorb the contents to the extent that we would like to. Whilst we are able to fill our waste bins with items that are clearly not wanted, a large amount of paper is still stored in most offices. Some of this may be as a result of legal requirements, where our actions can be subject to inspection and audit, and some may relate to the expectation or belief that we may need to refer to it at some time. Research has shown that only ten per cent of filed paper is ever referred to. Life could be so much simpler if we only knew in advance which ten per cent it was going to be.

Probably the most boring job in any office is the filing, and many of us can remember it being the first job we were given on starting work. Usually it was not up to date, and the filing cabinets were already full, so it took even longer to put new items into already bulging files. Data can become obsolete quite quickly these days, and the job of sifting through files to extract that which is obsolete needs doing more frequently. This can make paper filing systems very time consuming and expensive to operate. In addition, a filing cabinet takes up approximately two square metres of office space. This allows for the space it stands on, the space required for the drawers to open and the space for someone to stand in front of the open drawer. Also, the weight of paper in a full four-drawer filing cabinet is such that if there are a number of them to be sited together, professional advice may be necessary over their positioning with regard to the floor loading. One of the main disadvantages with a filing system is that the information can only be accessed or retrieved by a visit to the cabinet, either by the person requiring it, or by someone detailed for the task.

THINK POINT

Count up how many filing cabinets there are in your place of work and calculate how much space they require. Then find out what the rent is on the building, or what the usual local rent is for similar property usage, and calculate how much it costs per year in rent for your filing. To this you add the cost of the time it takes to do the filing and sifting of files. What economies can you make?

CARD SYSTEMS

Card systems are still very important, and until such time as everyone has access to a computer, they will continue to be. They are used to record data where much of the information is quite static. For example, the names, addresses and telephone numbers of subscribers, suppliers, members, customers etc. may not change much from year to year. However, adding new information to this system can be very time consuming, and anyone requiring the information must go to the file or get someone to do it for them. When information changes it can result in the whole card having to be re-typed or re-written.

One of the main uses of card systems has been in storage areas where stock cards or bin cards have been used for very many years. In this case the details of the stock item remain static, but the number held is amended with each delivery and withdrawal. These cards are then the basis of the periodical or perpetual system of stocktaking. Stocktaking is comparing the actual physical stock against what the records say should be there, and this is done at set intervals (periodical stocktaking); or a number of items is checked each day, so that all of the stock is checked over a twelve-month period (perpetual stocktaking). The value of the stock as part of the working capital of a business is now seen by most companies and organizations as being very important. As a result, a move to computerizing the stock-room is rapidly taking place, particularly where a large number of different items are held.

MICROFICHE

This is a system whereby information can be stored on a piece of film which can be read in a special viewer similar to the system used for viewing colour transparencies at home. A large number of pages of information, organized as a grid system, can be held on one piece of film. The required page of the information is found by moving the film within the viewer to the correct grid reference – if known – or sequentially, until it is located. The storage of the microfiche takes up very little space, but the viewer is similar in size to a small television set and needs to be accessible. This system is widely used for parts manuals and technical information on high-tech products, and sometimes for archival storage where space is a problem. It is, however, expensive to use for ordinary information storage purposes, as this requires a special camera system and entails the additional cost of having the film developed. Some of the viewers have the facility of being able to give a printout or hard copy of the information shown on the screen.

COMPUTERS

As a means of information storage and retrieval the computer is excellent, and deserves far more than the brief introduction we are able to give it here.

The most important features of the computer with regard to storing and retrieving information are:

1. vast amounts of information can be stored within even a small box of disks for a personal computer
2. the speed with which new information can be committed to memory
3. the movement of data from one file to another
4. the retrieval of information via the random access memory
5. the presentation of information in a variety of formats

If there is one area of business that competes with the jargon of the finance department it is computers. Advertisements for computers appear to be in a foreign language that is made up of figures and parts of words, or collections of letters mixed in with words. However, once we have a little learning on the subject, it is not as complex as it appears at first sight.

According to the dictionary, a computer is an apparatus for making calculations. This shows just how far computers have come in a relatively short space of time, because few of us would now think of a computer solely in those terms. It is true that making calculations can be a very important function of computers, particularly if you work for a bank or insurance company etc. It is, however, only a small part of what computers are now capable of, and does not relate to the subject of this chapter.

Computers are categorized according to their size. The first is the personal computer (PC), or micro-computer, which now comes in a variety of forms, including portable ones known as 'Notebooks'. Although the name suggests that these are for domestic use, they are very widely used in all sizes of business. Above these in size comes the mini-computers, which can be very powerful and are only used by businesses and organizations. Larger still are the mainframe computers which are used by very big companies and organizations and can cost many millions of pounds.

The personal computer

A typical personal computer (PC) consists of three main parts:

1. A system unit, which is a box containing the electronics etc.
2. A screen or monitor, which is similar to a television screen, and sits on top of the system unit.
3. A keyboard, which is similar to a typewriter keyboard, but has a number of additional keys.

Both the monitor unit and the keyboard are connected to the system unit by leads, although the lead from the monitor is usually built-in and cannot be seen.

The actual machine is referred to as the 'hardware', whereas the programs are called the 'software'.

Programs

Computers have to be told what to do, and this is achieved by loading into the computer a set of instructions called a 'program'. These instructions have to be in the special format or language that the computer has been built to understand. Programs can be written specifically for the user either by their own staff or by consultants, or they can be software packages which are written by specialist firms for different makes of computers. For many businesses and organizations the bought software package is the only economic option, but there is usually a good choice available. The programs are contained on disks, of which there are two basic sorts – hard disks and floppy disks.

Hard disks

Hard disks are usually contained within the systems unit and are permanently connected to the computer. They have a much higher storage capacity than a floppy disk and a number of programs can be kept permanently on them.

Floppy disks

A floppy disk does not appear as its name suggests. This is because the piece of thin plastic, which is the disk itself, is contained within a rigid plastic casing for protection and ease of use. The disk is covered with a magnetic coating which is similar to that of a normal cassette tape. The computer can read information from the disk or write information onto the disk in the same way as the play and record facilities of a cassette recorder. Programs held on floppy disk are accessed by inserting the disk containing the required program into a slot in the systems unit called the 'disk drive'. We then instruct the computer by means of the keyboard to load the particular program. What happens after that will depend very much on the type of program we have chosen, some of which are discussed below.

Word processing

Some computers are designed primarily to be word processors, but nearly all computers will run word-processing software. However, in addition to the three parts we discussed earlier, they must have a printer which is linked to the systems unit by a special lead. A word processor or computer using a word-processing package is so superior to a typewriter that it is surprising that typewriters are still produced. It has to be admitted, however, that the quality of print from a word processor or computer depends entirely on the quality of the printer connected to it. Some of the main advantages of using word processing include:

1 the ability to see what you have written on the screen before it is printed, and to make any necessary corrections and alterations
2 the ability to recall a standard letter to the screen and to personalize it for the recipient
3 the ability to have the spelling checked for you by the computer
4 being able to produce a similar letter for a number of people by typing it only once, but listing their names and addresses and any other required variables separately. The computer will then select the appropriate variable as it prints each letter – this is known as 'mail merge'
5 large documents, such as chapters of books, can be set up so that the title of the book and the title of each chapter appear on each page, and the pages are automatically numbered
6 there is no need to use carbon paper, as further copies are easily produced

Databases

A database is the computer's answer to the need for a filing system or card index. It enables you to store, organize, amend, add to, manipulate, move, delete and report on information with comparative ease. If we think back to the examples we used under card storage systems, we discussed the fact that we might wish to have the names, addresses and telephone numbers of subscribers, suppliers, members, customers etc. recorded. We also discussed the need for maintaining details of stocks of components, and so forth, in this way. All of these would be far more satisfactorily handled by a database program or software package on a personal computer or larger system. The ability to amend information without having to rewrite the whole file can save an enormous amount of time. All that is necessary is to bring the appropriate file onto the screen, delete the wrong information and type in the replacement. The remainder of the file which is correct is not affected.

Spreadsheets

A spreadsheet program is one which can lay out information in a preset format and automatically carry out calculations. For example, if we think back to the first section of this book, we had formats for balance sheets, budgets and cash flow forecasts. These could be preset on the computer so that as soon as we inserted the figures the mathematics would be done for us. Similarly, when John listed out the telephone costs for the four departments he could have preset the layout so that even the percentages were automatically calculated. The other key feature of the spreadsheet is that if it is linked to a suitable graphics software package, the results can be printed as graphs, pie charts, bar charts and so on.

In terms of the retrieval of information on the larger systems where information is stored on hard disk, a number of users, each with their own computer terminal, can have access to the same information, which in this case is stored centrally. If we contrast this with a row of filing cabinets, we can see the time saved by being able to access the required information without the need to move from our own work station. This type of system also allows users to communicate with one another or to send a message to a number of users at the same time, by electronic mail.

Inputting large amounts of information into the computer can be extremely time consuming and costly. However, the storage of information on the computer is very cheap, and the various facilities we have discussed above for using information that is computer-held usually justifies the cost. In terms of capital cost, the prices of computer hardware and software have fallen dramatically over recent years, and are now in a highly competitive market which favours the customer.

Data Protection Act 1984

Information about private individuals that you process on your computer may have to be registered under the Data Protection Act 1984.

Information that is only used in connection with personal, family or household matters or held for recreational purposes is exempt, but information that is held and processed for any other purpose, such as business or professional reasons, should be registered.

Guidelines on the Act are available from HM Stationery Offices.

British Standard BS 5750

In Charge, Managing Operations makes mention of the BS 5750 series of national standards for quality systems, which conform with the International Organization for Standardization (ISO) series ISO 9000. As these are general standards which are applicable to the quality systems for all products and services, they are of great importance to suppliers and purchasers alike, and will play an increasingly important part in our lives.

The reason we are including a section on the standards in this chapter on storing and retrieving information is that to achieve BS 5750, all of the operating and quality systems and procedures in a business or organization must be documented down to the last detail.

This documentation is at the very heart of the standards. Every laid-down procedure must be adhered to by all of the workforce, who must have copies of the parts which are relevant to their job readily accessible. After BS 5750 has been awarded, BSI inspectors will continue to monitor that the standards are being maintained. Any amendments to the documentation must have been made according to specific guidelines, and all of the various copies updated. Meticulous attention to detail and procedure is necessary to comply with the standards, and its storage and accessibility to all is crucial.

SUMMARY

Supervisory Management Standards:

Unit 7	Provide information and advice for action towards meeting organizational objectives
Element 7.1	Obtain, evaluate, record and store information
Element 7.2	Provide information and advice

In this chapter we have looked at the dangers and disadvantages of using our memories to store information without some form of back-up support.

We have examined the meaning and implications of GIGO – garbage in, garbage out.

Personal organizer systems have been discussed and an example of their usage given within our case study.

We have examined the problems and costs relating to the traditional systems of filing paper in cabinets, and have looked at the use of card systems.

The expense and specialist use of microfiche has been examined.

We have looked at the basic structure of the computer and discussed the use and benefits of various programs and software packages in terms of the storage and retrieval of information.

Mention has been made of the Data Protection Act 1984 and BS 5750, with regard to their influences on storing and retrieving information.

FURTHER READING

Ian Richards, *How to Use a Computer to Improve Your Business*. Graham and Trotman, 1989.

Chapter 11

Information in Interviews and Meetings

Supervisory Management Standards	
Unit 2	Contribute to the planning, monitoring and control of resources
Element 2.1	Plan the use of resources
Element 2.2	Monitor and control the use of resources
Unit 7	Provide information and advice for action towards meeting organizational objectives
Element 7.1	Obtain, evaluate, record and store information
Element 7.2	Provide information and advice

In chapter 9 we looked at ways of using numbers and presenting statistics and data in written form by using charts and graphs. In this chapter and the next one we are going to build on this and look at ways of communicating information to others both orally and visually, during interviews, meetings, talks, presentations, discussion groups etc.

INTERVIEWS

According to the dictionary definition, an interview is a face-to-face meeting with the purpose of conferring. This covers the informal one-to-one meeting as well as the more formal occasion, such as an appraisal interview. It makes no difference whether we have arranged to see our manager to discuss specific issues, such as the weekly output, request for a new machine etc., or whether it has been arranged as part of the formal company procedures; there are certain things that we should prepare in advance. It does not matter which of us has requested the meeting, the most important thing is that we are adequately prepared so that we can present our point of view in such a way that it is going to receive full consideration and stand the best possible chance of being accepted.

The great advantage of face-to-face communication is that you can more easily develop a rapport with the person or people present, and check their understanding of the points you are making. Any misunderstandings or disagreements can be far more easily dealt with when you can see their faces and gauge their reaction.

It is always best to try to arrange the meeting or interview for a time when you are least likely to be disturbed. Depending on the importance of the subject, it can be an advantage to arrange for it to be held in an interview room, if one is available. Obviously this will depend on whether your manager, if that is who the interview is with, is willing to move from his or her office, but if the subject is important it will do no harm to suggest it.

The next step is to think about who the interview is with and whether he or she absorbs information easily or likes to reflect on things before making a decision: it might prove advantageous to provide advance information in report form so that thought can be given to it prior to the interview. If something has gone wrong and you need an interview to explain the situation, giving advance information could provoke a storm without you having the opportunity to give your explanation right away. Obviously it would not be an advantage in this case.

If statistics are involved, decide how best you can present them to support your point of view. By this we mean finding the right layout (such as a bar chart, pie chart etc.) and providing the most appropriate calculations using the data. We certainly do not recommend that you distort the images in graph form as we discussed in chapter 9, because if you are found doing this, you will lose your credibility with your manager or whoever the interview is with.

Any communication of this sort is a negotiation exercise. If you want the other person to see your point of view you have to sell it to them. It can be that by providing data in a certain format your case is so obvious that it sells itself, but that may only be the way that you see it and the other person may see things differently. However hard we try, we tend only to see things from our point of view. You must therefore be prepared to sell how your ideas or views will benefit the unit, company, organization and the person you are talking to.

Case Note 8

In chapter 9 we met John Anderson, who is the senior clerk in the Accounts and Finance Department at Topicflex Ltd. You will recall that John had extracted the figures for the telephone bills of four of the head office departments, for his manager the company accountant, and that those for his own department had increased very considerably over the three years that he looked at. If John had sent the figures into his manager in the form that we have repeated in exhibit 11.1 there would almost certainly have been trouble, or at the very least a request for more specific information and explanations.

Exhibit 11.1 Topicflex Ltd head office, annual telephone costs in £000s

Department	199X	199Y	% increase on last year	199Z	% increase on last year
Accounts & Fin.	12	13	8.3	15	15.4
Personnel	14	15	7.1	16	6.7
Administration	6	7	16.7	9	28.6
Sales	43	45	4.7	46	2.2
Totals	75	80	6.7	86	7.5

In exhibit 11.1 the annual figures for each department had been rounded up to the nearest thousand pounds, which may have distorted the results. A more detailed analysis was therefore necessary, at least for the two departments that show the worst increases. We will concentrate on John's department, as he is responsible for the day-to-day running of it and therefore needed to be able to explain why the telephone bills had increased in this way.

The actual quarterly figures for the three years are given in exhibit 11.2.

John was quite sure that the increase was not due to the normal running of the department, and believed that it resulted from the very expensive telephone calls and faxes that he and the accountant had to send to Topicflex's subsidiary companies in other countries. He therefore analysed the figures further to separate out the overseas

Exhibit 11.2 Quarterly figures

Quarter	199X £	199Y £	199Z £
1	2,850	3,300	3,625
2	2,675	3,175	3,475
3	2,975	3,350	3,725
4	3,075	3,575	3,925
Totals	11,575	13,400	14,750

calls, and found that the results supported his suspicions.

He drew up a separate chart (exhibit 11.3) just for his department, and took both charts with him when he next had a meeting with his manager to discuss departmental issues. Because his manager is the company accountant, there was no need for John to show the figures in a more graphic form – an accountant is obviously accustomed to absorbing this sort of information at a glance. For other managers we could, in addition to the above charts, have shown the figures in bar chart form, with separate bars for the office portions and the international portions.

Exhibit 11.3 Accounts and Finance department telephone bills

	199X		199Y		199Z	
	Office	Intnatl	Office	Intnatl	Office	Intnatl
Quarter	£	£	£	£	£	£
1	2,425	425	2,575	725	2,725	900
2	2,225	450	2,375	800	2,550	925
3	2,450	525	2,625	725	2,825	900
4	2,525	550	2,700	875	2,900	1,025
Totals	9,625	1,950	10,275	3,125	11,000	3,750
% increase on previous year			6.7%	60.3%	7.1%	20.0%

MEETINGS

A meeting is described in the dictionary as 'an assembly of people for a purpose', or 'an organized assembly for the transaction of business'. So far in this chapter we have used the word 'meetings' as being synonymous with 'interviews'. However, we can see from the definitions that whilst every interview is a sort of meeting, meetings can be very much larger than interviews. The two dictionary definitions we have used here combine to give us two key elements for a meeting: it should be an *organized assembly* and it should have a *purpose*. Unfortunately, many so-called meetings appear to be lacking in both organization and purpose.

Most managers have to attend meetings, and the majority identify them as being the biggest time stealer that they have. On the other hand, the people who call and chair meetings regard them as essential to the running of the organization. Part of this divergence of opinion lies in the fact that many so-called meetings are in fact talks or lectures by the chairperson, during which the other attendees are required to sit, listen and say nothing. After having said everything to his or her personal satisfaction, the chairperson then believes that an important meeting has taken place and is totally oblivious to the feelings of the others.

Purpose

Every meeting should have a specific purpose, which should be communicated to all expected attendees. Regular daily, weekly, or monthly meetings which have no formal agenda are held because the group always meets at that time, have content created for the sake of filling the time. They are extremely costly and are usually of more value in terms of social contact than of business achievement. Some committees, by their very rules, have to meet periodically, but this is with the purposes of receiving reports from the officers and transacting the organization's business.

THINK POINT

Think of the meetings that you have attended recently and identify whether they were talks or lectures by the chairperson, or were regular meetings, where content had to be found to fill them. Then work out how long each attendee was away from their workplace as a result of attending the meeting, and what the cost of that time was in terms of salary plus any travelling and refreshment costs. (This only takes into account the actual cost to the company or organization or ignores how much they could have earned in profits by being at work.)

Annual general meetings

The annual general meeting is usually one form of regular meeting that must take place. Company annual general meetings are required by law and have a very formal agenda in a prescribed format. Most clubs have similar formal meetings on an annual basis. The conduct of these meetings is usually straightforward because it is laid down, and difficulties only arise when the prescribed procedures are not followed.

Calling a meeting

If you find that you have a good reason for calling a meeting, the first task is to decide who you need to attend and the dates between which it must be held. Do be careful how many people you have at a meeting, as the larger the number the less productive they can become. Clearly, adequate notice must be given both out of courtesy and to ensure that as many of the key people you need to attend are available to do so. At this stage it may be necessary to sound out a number of the key people as to their availability or the availability of their deputies, if this is acceptable. Several alternative dates may need to be offered to be able to obtain a satisfactory level of attendance. Where meeting facilities are limited, room availability will need checking before this takes place.

After you have decided upon the date, time and venue it is necessary to write to the proposed attendees requesting or inviting their attendance. In a work situation you may have to do this yourself, but ideally this should be done by the 'secretary', who will be responsible for taking the minutes, as in committee work. Often you will be chairing the meeting and acting as secretary, but if you can get help then you should do so. If the meeting is to have a sole purpose this should be clearly stated, including what is expected to be achieved, plus an indication of how long the meeting will take. If it is a talk or lecture rather than a meeting, then say so.

Where a meeting has a number of issues to be discussed it is important to involve the attendees in the agenda process. They must have the opportunity of suggesting items for discussion if you want their involvement and commitment. In this case, specify that agenda items must be received by you by a certain date, together with any advance reading which will need distributing to the attendees. Do specify that only items on the agenda will be discussed. (We will discuss the issue of 'any other business' later.) At the same time, each of the people you have invited should indicate whether they will be able to attend or who their deputy will be. The deadline that you choose for the agenda items and supporting information must allow sufficient time for you and the secretary to be able to finalize the agenda and send it, with any supporting documentation, to the attendees, in good time to permit them to prepare for the meeting. Either you or the secretary will amost certainly have to follow up a number of people who will have not responded by your deadline. This should only be on the basis of their attendance, as it should be made clear that they have missed the deadline for agenda items.

The items on the agenda should be prioritized so that if time should run out the least important items are the ones that are missed. It is all too easy to spend two hours discussing what type of drinks machine the canteen should have, only to find that you have no time left to decide on how you are going to staff a production line. However, if some people only need to attend for two or three items, do try to arrange these so that they are together. This might mean starting with them or making sure that you keep to your time-scale. You do not want to be sitting waiting for them to arrive, nor do you want them to have to sit through an hour of discussion which they are not interested in. If they are in the same building you can arrange for the secretary or an assistant to call them just before they are required.

Each item on the agenda should be given an allocation of time according to its importance, and this should be shown on the agenda. The agenda items should contain more than just a few words; they should fully explain what the subject is, what the discussion will cover and whether a decision is called for.

All too often people come to meetings with their own personal agendas. If the wording of your meeting agenda is insufficiently specific or you allow 'any other business', the meeting can be 'hijacked' and decisions on other issues will be manipulated without all interested parties being present.

If people are having to come long distances, do make sure that they are provided with good directions and information on parking etc., and indicate that tea or coffee will be available before the meeting, if this can be arranged.

Before the meeting

It is necessary to make sure that the room is booked and that any equipment required, such as flip charts and overhead projector and screen, will be available. Where attendees have asked for items on the agenda that will require some explanation, do encourage them to use visual aids, as these can very much reduce the length of time taken in explanation. Also, request that handouts are available where appropriate. Where people are coming from far away and require parking spaces, do make sure that these are booked, if this is possible, and advise reception or security of visitors' names if this is necessary. Any catering arrangements must also be made. On the day of the meeting arrange the room as you require it. The best format is a circular table, as everyone is then equal, but this is not often possible. Tables in the form of a square or rectangle can also be very effective. Make sure that additional copies of the agenda are available for those who have forgotten theirs, as well as notepaper and pencils or ballpoint pens.

The meeting

Always start your meetings on time. It is wrong to penalize those who are on time by making them wait for latecomers, and it only encourages people to be late in future. Thank everyone for coming, announce any administrative arrangements (such as any breaks for refreshments) and start on the first item, which will be the acceptance of the minutes of the previous meeting, if there was one for this group.

Your role as chairperson is more that of coordinator than of being in charge. There is a tendency for chairpeople to feel that they must have the most to say, but this is entirely wrong. The role is very much one of facilitating the interchange between the various members to ensure that all worthwhile comments are heard, and that agreement is reached on the basis of full information. Chairperson – or coordinator, which is a more descriptive title – is not an easy role, as the people attending the meeting will include many different sorts who will present different problems in terms of your approach. There will be those who are talkative and who want to ramble on, often going off onto other subjects, and you will need to interrupt to bring them back to the subject. Then summarize what they have said before passing the subject to someone else. Some will be shy and afraid of speaking up or drawing attention to themselves; you will need to ask them for their comments or their views, but do use easy questions and be sure to thank them for their contribution. The know-all type is a familiar figure at a meeting, and it is usually best to let the remainder of the group sort this person out, and for you to come in and summarize the majority view. There are many other types, and experience will help you to deal with them, just as you have to deal with these types in other parts of your job.

Do keep an eye on the time and your schedule for the meeting, although you must be prepared to be flexible if you are into a really important discussion. At the end of each agenda item summarize what has been agreed, who is to take action, and by when. Never use the expression 'as soon as possible', as this tends to mean the same as the Spanish 'mañana', meaning tomorrow – and tomorrow never comes! These summaries will help you or the secretary, if you have one, to be sure that your notes on what has been agreed are correct. At the end of the meeting agree the date of the next or subsidiary meetings, and thank everyone for their attendance and contributions.

The minutes

The record of what has been discussed and agreed is essential to the meeting process. Without it, in many cases, you might as well not have bothered to hold the meeting at all. Even one week after the meeting, recollections of what took place will be totally different. It is therefore important that the secretary writes up the minutes in draft form and agrees them with the chairperson within two or three days, and that the final draft is sent to the attendees immediately after that.

The minutes should have a separate column on the right-hand side in which to indicate who is to take action, what the action is and by when it is to be completed.

The most important things to remember about meetings are:

1 everyone should know the purpose of the meeting
2 ample notice should be given
3 each person who is to attend should have the opportunity of contributing to the agenda
4 the agenda should be prioritized on the basis of importance
5 time should be allocated for each agenda item
6 the meeting should be coordinated to ensure that everyone has an opportunity to contribute
7 the timetable for the meeting should be adhered to as far as possible
8 accurate minutes, with an action column showing who is to do what and by when, should be sent out less than a week after the meeting

If you follow these guidelines you will have successful meetings that people will be happy to attend. In addition, your reputation within the company or organization will be enhanced, as meetings are often the subject of discussion.

SUMMARY

Supervisory Management Standards:

Unit 2	Contribute to the planning, monitoring and control of resources
Element 2.1	Plan the use of resources
Element 2.2	Monitor and control the use of resources
Unit 7	Provide information and advice for action towards meeting organizational objectives
Element 7.1	Obtain, evaluate, record and store information
Element 7.2	Provide information and advice

In this chapter we have looked at ways of communicating information to others in interviews and meetings.

We discussed the benefit of the interview as a vehicle for communication between two or more people, during which rapport can be established.

We commented on the fact that as a result of being able to see the other person and gauging their reaction to the issues, their understanding and agreement can be checked and discussed, where necessary.

The whole process of running meetings was discussed, as well as the reasons why many meetings are considered to be a waste of time.

We looked at how to organize a meeting, how to run a meeting and how to record a meeting.

Chapter 12

Making Presentations

Supervisory Management Standards	
Unit 7	Provide information and advice for action towards meeting organizational objectives
Element 7.2	Provide information and advice

We are required more and more in our jobs to make presentations to groups of subordinates in team briefings, or to peers, managers and customers. Unless we have received some instruction on making presentations, the first few times can be terrifying, and we marvel at the self-confidence of those who can stand up in front of others without any evidence of being nervous. However, even the most experienced of speakers will admit to some inner tensions at the start of a talk or presentation and often seem surprised that the audience is unaware of this. If you ask a number of individuals to write down a list of the feelings and nervous symptoms that they were conscious of when they last made a presentation, you will nearly always find that all of them have very similar things listed. These are likely to include butterflies in the stomach, feeling sick, dry mouth, sweaty palms etc.

As in the case of the interview, proper preparation is essential. It is much easier to speak on a subject that you are completely familiar with and where you have anticipated what the questions are likely to be.

In preparing what you are going to say and how you are going to say it, you first need to know who your audience is going to be. This needs to include how many there will be, what level of seniority they have in relation to your own, what sort of age group they are and what level of knowledge they have of your subject. In addition, it is always important to know why they will be present – is it voluntary or have they been sent? Sometimes people have travelled a long way to be present, and it is necessary to be aware of this.

If you have been invited to speak, rather than deciding to do so within the work environment as a part of your job, it is necessary to make sure that you are properly briefed as to the exact requirements by whoever has asked you. That person is also usually the best person from whom to obtain information on the audience listed in the previous paragraph.

When you have the information on your audience you are then in a position to decide at what level to pitch your presentation, and to choose the most appropriate content.

THINK POINT

Think of the last talk or presentation that you attended. Was the content appropriate for the audience? Did you learn anything of interest to you, and did it hold your attention throughout?

Most speakers would agree that it is usually easier to make an internal presentation than an external one. An internal presentation has the advantages of usually being in surroundings with which you are familiar, and of having an audience that is known to you. An external presentation in a strange place, with unfamiliar equipment and an unknown audience can be far more daunting.

In planning your presentation much will depend on how much time you have been given both for the presentation and for questions afterwards. It will also depend on how essential it is that you make the presentation, in the light of the other pressures on your time. An afternoon presentation on one of your hobbies to the local pensioners' club is likely to be less important than getting the work out on time. Whereas a presentation to a group of supervisors and managers in your company or organization on how, with their cooperation, you could increase profits, would be seen as essential.

If there are other speakers you will need to know what subjects they are covering and in what depth. There is nothing worse than sitting waiting for your turn to speak and listening to the other speakers using up your topic. If you are only required to attend for part of the time, you need to know how early you need to be there and when you can test any audio-visual equipment that you need to use. If you are not sure of where the venue is, do make sure that you are provided with a map or really good instructions, and know where you can park.

The layout of the room is very important according to how formal you want the occasion to be. If numbers are reasonably small and you want to create as much discussion and interaction as possible, then an informal arrangement is best, whereas if you are speaking to a large number of people, a more formal theatre or classroom style will be necessary. Obviously, if you are only one of a number of speakers then it will be difficult to alter the seating arrangements.

Do make sure that if you are using audio-visual equipment that the people at the back of the room and at the sides can see and hear. The lighting very often needs to be experimented with to ensure that it is at a comfortable level for the audience and does not reflect off any screen that you are using. Very often the controls for the air conditioning and central heating are sited outside the room or are concealed within it, and it is therefore necessary to check these out in advance.

THE STRUCTURE

After you have satisfied yourself as to the brief you have been given or, if this is your idea, what you are seeking to achieve, it is then necessary to build the skeleton of your presentation. To do this you will need to jot down everything that you need to cover, would like to cover or might cover, in rough headings. These can then be sorted into a logical sequence. At this stage it will be necessary to discard a number of items, as most speakers have a tendency to have too much material as a result of the fear of not having enough. This results in many presentations going on far too long and the main message being lost in trivia. It is better to make three or four strong points which will be remembered than to send your audience away unsure of what your main theme was. At this stage you will need to decide what sort of data and information you will need to reinforce and support your arguments. Do be careful that you have a logical sequence to your presentation so that the audience are able to follow the 'story-line'. If you do this it will be much easier for them to understand you and to remember what you have said.

How to start

The way to start a presentation depends very much on your audience, how well you know them and on the occasion. It could be that the moment you stand up you will immediately have their undivided attention. On other occasions it will be necessary to 'capture' them by telling a joke, making some outrageous remark or asking a question. If the length of the session you are running is to last a half day or more, and the number is less than around sixteen, it can be very useful to get them to introduce themselves and their interests in the subject. Obviously you will also need to introduce yourself and your interest and knowledge of the subject. This is the time to let the audience know when you would prefer to answer questions and whether there will be a handout.

Often, giving them a summary of how you are going to tackle your subject can be effective. This is very much in line with the army non-commissioned officer style of giving a talk: 'Tell them what you are going to tell them, tell them, then tell them what you have told them.' This gives a beginning, a middle and an end which reinforces the message.

The middle

In following your sequence or 'story-line', after your beginning must come the middle. This is where you have to achieve your purpose and sell the ideas and concepts that you are describing to them. You must be very clear as to what your objective is, and be sure that what you are telling them will achieve it. The key word for this section is focus. Your enthusiasm for your subject is of great importance and will enliven the talk. Anecdotes based on your experience can add to the interest, but do be careful that you do not go off at tangents and blur the message you are trying to put across. It should be possible for anyone in the audience to be able to write down exactly what your purpose was and what the structure of your talk consisted of. If you are trying to sell a particular outcome, then the structure of your argument should lead your audience to your logical conclusion. If there are some obvious drawbacks to your proposals, such as cost or longer working hours, then deal with these early in this part of your presentation. Otherwise, some of your audience will think of them and will be concentrating on how they can raise the issues during question time rather than listening to what you are saying.

The ending

The last part of any presentation is of great importance in terms of getting the message across. Surveys have shown that people tend to remember some of the beginning, the outstanding parts from the middle, but most of the ending. If you want the audience to go away and do something – such as looking at ways of cutting costs or answering the telephone more quickly – then say so. You may want to appeal to their conscience over something, or you may make a recommendation. The most important closing of all is to summarize what you have said so that they have your main objective as their final thought.

PREPARATION

Preparing your notes

After you have roughed out your presentation and constructed your story-line, which is then matched by the audio-visual aids you will choose, it is time to prepare your notes, aide-mémoire or memory jogs. These can be in a variety of forms, and the one you choose is a matter of your personal preference and experience.

Writing it out in full

Many people, when they are starting to make presentations, like the comfort of having their script written out in full so that they overcome the fear of drying up or forgetting what they were going to say. This can have the advantage of ensuring that nothing gets missed out and can be particularly useful for certain very technical topics.

Unfortunately, it can result in a boring presentation if all the audience can see is the top of the presenter's head. It is questionable in this case whether there is any advantage to listening to someone read the paper to them as opposed to being given a copy to read for themselves.

If you are going to have your presentation written out in full, do make sure that it is typed in double spacing on cards or on as thick a paper as possible. Do be careful to use the words that you would speak as opposed to the words you use in writing. Only use one side of the paper and do make sure that they are numbered. Use a highlighter to highlight key words so that you are able to speak from memory at times. This will then make it possible for you to be able to look at and make as much eye contact with your audience as possible. If you are proposing to use full notes that are typed out onto paper, do try to make sure that a lectern is available, as any slight shaking of your hands will be exaggerated if you hold your papers.

Try to have certain parts that you are more confident with, such as anecdotes, just in key word form, as this will enable you to use more eye contact.

Notes

These can be in a number of forms and vary according to how full or brief they are. Small note cards can be a usful form, as they fit into the palm of the hand and do not restrict the speaker's movements. They either need to be numbered, or it can be useful to punch a hole in the top left-hand corner and to put some form of ring through the holes, which will keep them together but still enable them to be turned over easily. The use of key words can be very important here. Your notes may cover each key point, plus any quotations or technical points that you prefer not to trust to memory, plus your starting and closing comments. The great advantage of this method is that it enables you to build and maintain rapport with your audience through eye contact.

No notes

This is a style that is appropriate for experienced speakers who have good knowledge of their subject. Even then it can result in important points being missed and the talk appearing unstructured, as there is a greater danger of wandering off the main subject. It is also far more difficult to get the timing right.

Whichever of these note systems you choose to use, do make sure that they include copies of any overhead projector slides that you are proposing to use. This will avoid the tendency of turning away from your audience to read off the screen or standing in the way of your audience whilst trying to read off the slide on the overhead projector.

Rehearsal

When you have prepared your notes or script it is then necessary to practise delivering your talk. To begin with, this is best done on your own in front of a mirror. After you have tried this a number of times and are reasonably happy with your notes, if you have a video camera available try filming yourself. From this you will be able to see to what extent you are looking up from your script, whether you are varying the pitch and tone of your voice and whether you are varying the speed that you are speaking at. It will show whether you are speaking too quickly or too deliberately. It may also make you aware of any mannerisms and habits that could distract your audience – such as fidgeting with things or using particular words too much, like 'right', 'actual' and 'actually'.

If you do not have access to a video camera, ask a friend or colleague to listen to you and to give honest feedback. Obviously it is necessary to choose someone whose opinion you trust to do this for you. If possible, try to practise at least once in the room that you are going to use, or one of a similar size, as this is likely to be very different from your lounge and will require greater projection of the voice if you are going to be heard by all.

AUDIO-VISUAL AIDS

In planning what you are going to say, we have talked in terms of having a logical sequence or story-line. It is equally important that the audio-visual aids that you use to support your presentation follow your story-line and are an integral part of it. All too often in presentations elaborate slides are shown which do nothing for the presentation, or detract from it. One excellent way of planning your visual aids is to use the story board approach which is used in the television and film industry. Here a sequence of drawings is made to summarize the development of the story through visual images. To use this technique for planning your visual aids for a presentation, you need to put copies of the ones that you propose using onto a large sheet of paper to see whether they make the same story as you are using in your talk, or whether people might go away remembering the wrong message. If the story is wrong or there are gaps in it, you will need to change some or add others. Do be careful about having too many of them though. All too often the whole of a presentation can look like a slide show.

1 Three-dimensional objects

The best visual aid of all is the actual object that you are talking about (or a model of it). If you are explaining a new component to assemblers, or how a joint works to student nurses, or how to use a fax machine, actually seeing the object or a working model will speak volumes and is more likely to be remembered. It also gives you something that you can demonstrate and you will find this much easier to talk about. Do be careful about using small objects, as they may not be easily seen by all of the audience and passing them round can take a surprisingly long time. Inviting the audience to have a look at them after question time can be a useful way out of this.

2 Posters, diagrams and placards

The advantages of these are that they can be prepared without the need for specialist equipment. They are easily transported and put on display. They can brighten up a dull room and can be a talking point whilst the audience is waiting for the presentation to begin. You do, however, require access to the room in advance to put them up, and they can distract the audience if they are left up throughout the presentation.

3 Flip chart pads

Flip chart sheets can be prepared beforehand or used *in situ*. A wide variety of coloured felt-tip marker pens are available for use with them. Most training rooms and conference halls have them available, and also the stands to go with them. They can be displayed on the walls around the room as your talk or series of talks builds up. Do avoid writing too much on one sheet, as the impact will be lost. If you are going to use a flip chart whilst you are talking, do make sure in advance that there are enough blank sheets left on the pad, as they have a habit of being down to the last one. Also, be careful to keep the amount of writing to a minimum as it necessitates you turning your back on your audience, and you cannot communicate and build rapport like that. To a certain extent this can be overcome when using a flip chart stand of the easel type by standing at the side of it, so that the side of you is turned towards your audience rather than your back. This position makes it far easier to maintain rapport and eye contact, as you can turn towards your audience between each of the entries you make. Obviously this technique is not possible where the flip chart is mounted on the wall.

4 Chalkboards and whiteboards

These are widely available in training and conference rooms but their usage during a talk or presentation, as in the use of wall-mounted flip charts, results in turning your back on your audience to an extent. Any spelling errors are instantly apparent to the audience but not to the presenter! There are electronic whiteboards that are capable of printing a paper copy of what has been written on the board. Do ensure that you use non-permanent marker pens on whiteboards and that the sort you are proposing to use is compatible with that make of board. Boards can be permanently damaged by the wrong sort of marker. Chalkboards are strongly associated with school days and can irritate adult audiences.

5 Flannel or felt boards

These are quite easily constructed by stretching a piece of felt over a piece of hardboard. They are portable and can be used to build up a picture as the talk progresses by using sections mounted on pieces of card which have a velcro pad stuck to the backs. One possible drawback can be that, unless the quality of the print and the images are professional, they can be reminiscent of Sunday school.

6 Magnetic boards

Magnetic boards are used in a similar way to felt or flannel boards, but are more effective and have a more modern image. However, they have the additional disadvantage of being heavy to transport.

7 Pin boards

These are paper-covered boards which are used by pinning paper and card to them. This makes them sound somewhat crude: however, if the audience is small and the session you are running is an interactive one, they can be used so that members of the group can add their ideas. This can make a session quite dynamic, and once the board has been purchased it is very cheap to use.

8 Overhead projectors

Overhead projectors (OHPs) are now one of the most frequently-used forms of visual aids. Research has shown that statistical data presented on slides in the most appropriate format is extremely persuasive.

The acetate slides for overhead projectors are of two main sorts: those that can be used in a photocopier to print the required image onto them, and those that will melt in a photocopier and require an engineer to restore it to use.

Special pens are available for writing on the slides and, therefore, besides their initial preparation, they can be added to during a presentation. The screen is bright and the lights can be left on in the room during its use to assist with note taking. The pictures can be projected to a good size and the projector can easily be put out of the way when it is not required. The speaker can, and should, remain facing the audience whilst using an overhead projector. The slides should be mounted in cardboard frames for ease of handling, and pieces of card can be stuck to the frame with tape to enable parts of the slide to be revealed at different times.

It is essential to ensure that a spare bulb is available. Some machines have a spare bulb that can be brought into use when necessary by flicking a switch, but this needs checking in advance. Some machines can be quite noisy because they are usually fan cooled.

When using an overhead projector, it is essential to position the screen in such a way that you are not obstructing any of the audience's view of the screen. Many people have a tendency to turn and look at the screen when using an overhead projector, and even to read from it. This should be avoided, for as in the case of the chalkboard and whiteboard, you cannot communicate with your audience through the back of your head. When using an overhead projector do try to remember to switch it off and to remove your last slide as soon as you have moved on in your story-line, as it can be distracting.

Try not to use too many overhead slides. A ten-minute presentation should not have more than four, and if you are speaking for much longer the rate of use should go down to one every four or five minutes at most. When you are making a series of presentations do make sure that you number your slides in the order that you intend to use them, in case they are dropped or knocked over.

The main faults with the way in which overhead projector slides are prepared include the number of words used and the size of the lettering. Slides should be used to summarize and emphasize, and as such should contain no more than five headings consisting of a maximum of three or four words each. These must be in considerably larger print than normal typewriter size, and should be in a style that is easily read from the back of the room by someone with less than perfect eyesight. Slides are also an effective means of displaying simple statistics. Any figures and writing should be visible from the back of the room. However, this can be overcome if the point being made about the figures is obvious as a result of the use of pie charts, bar charts etc., and is then supported by a handout at the end of the presentation which gives greater detail.

9 Slide projectors

The great advantage of the use of a slide projector is that photographic images can be displayed. This is not possible with most other forms of visual aid we have looked at. A very wide range of material can be shown and a sequence or story-line built up. The very sharp, bright images focus audience attention very effectively, either on a large screen or through a television-type monitor. A number of companies specialize in producing high-quality slides to customer requirements for presentations.

The disadvantages of slide projection include the fact that the room must have effective blackout facilities, and this makes note taking impossible. The slides can be time consuming to prepare, and unless the projector is remotely controlled, additional assistance is necessary. This system also lacks flexibility, as once the projection has started it cannot be added to or changed. As in the case of the overhead projector, a spare bulb is essential.

10 Audio tapes

Audio tapes are very good for demonstrating noise levels, particular sounds, music etc., but have a very limited usage on their own for normal presentation work. A small cassette recorder is inadequate for playing tapes to an audience in a room larger than the normal domestic living room, so more powerful equipment is usually necessary. The main disadvantage is that the audio tape only makes use of the sense of hearing.

11 Slide projection with audio tape

This can be a very effective means of presentation, but needs to be professionally prepared. It is expensive to make, although much cheaper than commissioning a professional video. The disadvantages discussed with regard to the slide projector apply here also.

12 Video

This is a very powerful method of presentation which, perhaps because of its similarities with television, audiences are comfortable with. It is vivid, colourful and can arouse emotions. It is very important that you properly introduce the video that you are going to use before switching the equipment on, and summarize the key points afterwards. Do check in advance that the video tape that you propose to use is of the same format as the equipment that is being provided, as many company facilities are UMATIC instead of the more familiar VHS.

There are a large number of pre-recorded tapes available, but nearly all of them run for at least twenty-five minutes, so it will be necessary to choose particular sections, depending on the length of time that you have available. Pre-recorded tapes can be expensive both to buy and to rent. Self-produced video tapes require editing facilities, and even then can appear crude to an audience familiar with television standards.

The disadvantages also include the fact that it is extremely expensive to commission a professionally made video. As in the case of the slide projector, taking notes is not possible because the room requires blackout curtains or blinds and the lights out.

13 Handouts

Handouts are an excellent way of summarizing and reinforcing your message, and are essential if you want your audience to pass the information on to others. They save the need for going into too much technical detail during your presentation, and enable you to keep your visual aids simple to improve impact. They do need to be prepared carefully, in a bold format with subheadings for ease of reference, and checked thoroughly. They should be collated, bound or stapled where necessary, and given out at the end of the question time. The audience should be advised in advance what will be covered by the handout so that they know what notes to take. If the handout is given out at the start or during the presentation, then people will read it instead of listening.

14 Other forms

Other forms of visual aids are worked off images stored on computer, and include data projectors and talking walls etc., but access to these facilities is very limited.

For all of the audio-visual aids we have discussed which are powered by electricity, it is essential that you:

1. check the whereabouts, number and type of power points available in the room
2. check the model and type of equipment that is available, and that it has been booked
3. carry an extension lead with you which has two power points on it
4. if you are going to make presentations on a frequent basis and in different venues, it is worth investing in a variety of adaptors for power points

The number of different types of audio-visual aids that you use depends on the length of your presentation. A ten-minute presentation should preferably only have one type, whereas a twenty-minute one could have two. However, it does not matter for how long you are speaking, three different types should be the maximum in any one session, otherwise you will appear to be jumping around from one piece of equipment to another.

AT THE PRESENTATION

Make sure that you are suitably dressed for the occasion. A presentation is a formal or at least semi-formal occasion, and a business-like appearance can add authority to the speaker. Always arrive in good time and make the various checks and preparations we have already discussed. Ensure that you are provided with a glass and some water as the throat can become dry if you are nervous. In the event of something going wrong, do make light of it by the use of humour (if possible) and try to stay calm. If the problem is your host's responsibility, sit down and wait for it to be resolved.

AFTER THE PRESENTATION

Do make sure that you clear up all of your notes and equipment. In particular, if you have used a video do make sure that you have rewound it and removed it from the player. This is often the time when a member of the audience, who was afraid to ask a question in front of the others, will come up to you to ask it. Put all of your materials away carefully as you may require them again. Later, when you are on your own, make notes of how you feel the presentation went, what you have learned from it, what you would do differently if you have to make another presentation.

THINK POINT

How would you, as a supervisor, carry out a team briefing, of your work team, on a new system which would change the way in which you operate?

Case Note 9

Karen Wells of Wells (Plumbers) Ltd decided that one of the problems she had in scheduling her work related to the number of emergency call-outs she received in respect of frozen and burst pipes. Whilst these were costed so that the work was profitable, they involved having to leave new installation work, which often annoyed customers. Also, burst pipes frequently caused damage to customers' furniture and property. Karen felt that the proper way round this problem was to try to educate customers about having their pipes insulated. She therefore decided that she would give talks at the local clubs on the subject: a form of advertising that would help to bring in additional domestic work for the company.

She discussed the matter with Sue, and they agreed that the Women's Institute branches, Young Wives clubs and Senior Citizens clubs would be the right sort of places and were always looking for speakers. Colin and Jack were both in favour of the idea, but were glad that Karen had volunteered to do it rather than asking them.

Karen contacted the secretary of the Women's Institute in her area, who was delighted with the idea, and they arranged a date in six weeks' time. This allowed the secretary to include it in her programme and advise the members, and Karen to prepare how and what she was going to say.

The only previous experience Karen had had of making a presentation was during her training at college to become a plumbing and central heating engineer. All of her class had to make two ten-minute presentations to the others on different aspects of the work. Karen's presentations had gone well, but she was apprehensive about speaking to an audience whom she did not know until Sue pointed out that none of the audience would know as much about the subject as she did.

She decided that she would need some good visual aids to be able to explain her subject, and so she asked Colin and Jack if they would make her a very large doll's house arrangement which showed the plumbing in the loft as well as the rest of the house, including inside the garage and an outside tap. The model house needed to be in sections so that it could be quickly built up in the hall and fit in one of the vans.

She decided that she should aim initially at speaking for thirty to forty minutes, and then answer questions, so that the whole presentation would be about an hour in length. After she had roughed out everything that she wanted to say, she realized that she had far too much. The anecdotes that resulted from her experience, plus those of Jack and Colin, needed pruning, as they would have filled the whole of the time. When she was satisfied with the content she transferred the key words onto small cards and started to practise. By this time it was two weeks before the presentation and the model house (which, when built up, measured two metres square) was ready. After she was reasonably satisfied, she asked Sue to listen to her and to give her feedback.

On the evening of the presentation Karen and Sue arrived at the hall before anyone else, erected the model and then put sheets over it. They made sure that they had an adequate stock of their business cards available and put out on a side table leaflets of new bathroom suites and central heating systems. They had previously rubber stamped all of the leaflets with their company name and telephone number.

About twenty members attended the evening, and Karen was to speak after all of the club's other activities for the evening were over. Having to wait to speak added to her nervousness, but when they stopped for a cup of tea immediately before she was going to speak she found that they were all very friendly and seemed really interested in her job.

After tea, when they had all resumed their places, the chairlady introduced Karen and Sue, who had joined her on the platform. When Karen stood up to speak she first poured herself a glass of water to calm herself and because her mouth had become dry. She then explained how and why she had decided to become a plumber and central heating engineer, and then went on with the main part of her presentation. The anecdotes went down extremely well, as they were based on everyday happenings with which the audience could identify. When she had finished speaking, she found that she had taken over an hour because she had only referred to her notes for the main headings once she had got into her stride. As the audience was interested and it had been going well she had added extra material. The questions went on for another forty minutes, and the chairlady had to cut them short as the caretaker wanted to close up.

Both Karen and Sue agreed that the evening had gone extremely well. During the following week they received two enquiries for quotations for installation work as a result of the evening, plus phone calls from the secretaries of two other Women's Institutes, inviting Karen to speak.

SUMMARY

Supervisory Management Standards:

Unit 7	Provide information and advice for action towards meeting organizational objectives
Element 7.2	Provide information and advice

In this chapter we have taken an in-depth look at presentations and how to make them.

We have looked at the need for a thorough preparation, which includes knowledge of the audience, structuring what to say, rehearsing the presentation and setting out the room.

We identified the need for a good opening, followed by a logically structured main section and a strong ending.

The whole range of visual aids was discussed, together with the various ways of preparing notes or memory jogs.

We discussed the need for appraising how the presentation had gone, and identifying the things that we would do differently in future.

Chapter 13
Writing Reports

Supervisory Management Standards	
Unit 2	Contribute to the planning, monitoring and control of resources
Element 2.1	Plan the use of resources
Element 2.2	Monitor and control the use of resources
Unit 7	Provide information and advice for action towards meeting organizational objectives
Element 7.1	Obtain, evaluate, record and store information
Element 7.2	Provide information and advice

Very often at work we are asked by our managers to write a paper or a report on a particular issue. Sometimes it is because they do not have time to discuss the item or problem with us. Sometimes considerable research will be necessary to collect all of the information that is necessary, before conclusions can be drawn and decisions made.

Reports can best be categorized by their size. A relatively short report of between one thousand and two thousand words will need a simple structure to it, as it can be read at a single attempt by most readers. They might choose to skim read it first to check their interest in the topic, but it does not require the more elaborate structure that is necessary with a report of over three thousand words. Some of the approaches to report writing are the same whatever the size, and it will help if we look at these aspects before we go on to consider them individually.

When we are asked to write a report, there are a number of very basic points that we need to cover.

For a start, we need to know who is going to read the report. For example, if John Anderson at Topicflex Ltd was asked by his manager, the company accountant, to write a report on the allocation of costs of the head office, he might write a quite technical paper full of accountants' jargon on the assumption that only his manager wanted it. If he later found that it was to be copied to all department heads, managers and supervisors, he might have wished that he had made further enquiries of his manager at the start. He now probably needs to rewrite it so that it is suitable for this wider readership.

John's next problem might be that he and his manager had both understood different things by 'the allocation of costs of the head office'. John may have understood his manager to mean the way in which the overhead costs relating to the whole of the head office function are divided out between the different manufacturing sites and wholesale outlets. His manager's intention may have been for a report on how costs are allocated to the departments within the head office, such as the basis on which the rent and rates are divided up or the electricity and heating bills etc. If John had only written a short report of, say, fifteen hundred words on the subject, where he had nearly all of the information, he might have muttered a few well-chosen expletives under his breath and have got on with the new report. If, on the other hand, he had spent several weeks researching information and had written a report of, say, seven thousand words, then the situation would be very different. The cost of the wasted report would be high and a further long period would be required before the new report could be ready. That time might not have been available.

From these two examples, which are all too typical of the problems of communication within companies and organizations, we can see that it is essential that whenever we are asked to write a report it is necessary to clarify exactly what the other person has in mind. It may well be that the request has been made by someone higher than the person who has passed it to you. Your manager, or the person who has passed the request to you, may not have even thought about it, other than to consider who they can get to do it. It will then be necessary for either you, this other person or your manager, if he or she has authorized it to be given to you, to go to that higher authority to obtain clarification.

Whilst it is extremely frustrating to find that you have wasted your time in doing the wrong report, the cost implications can be far more serious. The time taken in doing the report has an obvious cost but there is also what is termed the 'opportunity cost', which is the value of the work you could have done instead. The delay in getting the right information to the manager concerned could be expensive, as could the cost of his or her time in explaining again what it was that he or she actually wanted.

It is always best if the person who is required to write the report is briefed on it by the person who actually requires it. The more times the message is passed down the more it can become corrupted.

When you are briefed on a request for a report, always ask questions to ensure that you are both thinking of the same thing.

1 Try to find out what the background circumstances are to the request for the report.
2 Ask what the purpose of the report is.
3 Enquire who the report is primarily for and who else is likely to read all or parts of it.
4 Ask what sort of information the reader will expect to find in the report, and how much knowledge they already have.
5 Find out what they expect the outcome to be.
6 You also need to know what the time limits are both in terms of the draft and the finished report. Also, whether the sponsor of the report wants progress reports on it.
7 Ask what level of confidentiality, if any, the report has, and who it may be discussed with.
8 Enquire what authority you have to access sources of information that are normally not available to you.
9 Where the project will involve the conditions of service of others, you will need to know whether they have been informed or consulted.
10 Enquire what support, such as typing, is available.
11 Enquire as to the size of the budget, if the project/report/investigation is a particularly long one.

If you are only being asked for a relatively short report, you can now go to the planning stage.

TERMS OF REFERENCE (TOR)

For a major report, when you have satisfied yourself that you know the answers to the above, go away and write down a description of the task or tasks. You will need to word this as specifically as is necessary to identify the task, but without so restricting yourself that possible alternative solutions must be omitted. In identifying the tasks, it is usually helpful to list and number objectives and put them into a logical sequence.

Many reports are about proposals for doing things differently, and a logical sequence would be:

1 to describe the present arrangements
2 to analyse the advantages and disadvantages of the present arrangements
3 to describe alternative method(s)
4 to list and analyse the advantages and any disadvantages of the alternative method(s)
5 to identify any problems in implementing a change from the current method to an alternative method
6 to prepare a cost/benefit analysis

You should include a general description of the sort of information that you believe will be necessary, and how you propose to go about collecting it. You will need to indicate how long the tasks will take you to complete, or any deadlines that have been negotiated or requested.

You will now need to type this out, stating that is what you have been requested to do and by whom. If support from others has been negotiated and authorized, then this should also be stated. Then obtain the signature of the person who requested the report to this document as this will confirm that you are on the right track. It will also form your authority for obtaining certain information that otherwise might be barred to you. This document is referred to as your 'terms of reference', and it is only after you have obtained this that a suitable title should be agreed, as this should reflect the content of the report.

PREPARATION AND PLANNING

The next task is to plan how you are going to tackle the report. This will depend on when the report is required and how much time you realistically have available to do it. This means that you will have to schedule your time and perhaps some work of a lesser importance will have to be put off until this report has been completed. The use of a Gantt chart, as discussed in *Managing Operations*, would be helpful to plan the time available for the task.

The largest amount of time will be taken up by research and the collection of data and information. The actual writing only takes a relatively short time once the collection of information is complete. It is quite possible to write five or six thousand words in a day, although three thousand is more normal on a technical subject.

Our starting-point is to look at our 'terms of reference' and to break the subject down into its component parts in order to identify the various topics and areas for investigation. We then need to identify the sources of information on each of those areas. These might be technical data from suppliers, textbooks from the library, data from another department, or someone who has the experience and knowledge we require etc. Our first investigation on some of the topics or areas might be to find out the sources of information.

For each of the main areas of our subject we will need to decide how much detail we need to go into. This will be influenced by the purpose of the report and our terms of reference. To assist us with this, we need to think about the questions or queries which will need answering. These will be at different levels, as general questions on a subject will need to be followed by others that become increasingly specific, until we could be dealing with the merest detail. Often when we are talking about a study or investigation we use the expression 'in-depth', and figure 13.1 shows a sort of organizational structure of questions. We need to use this sort of basis for each of the topics we have identified from our terms of reference.

Obviously the questions on detail can be many-layered.

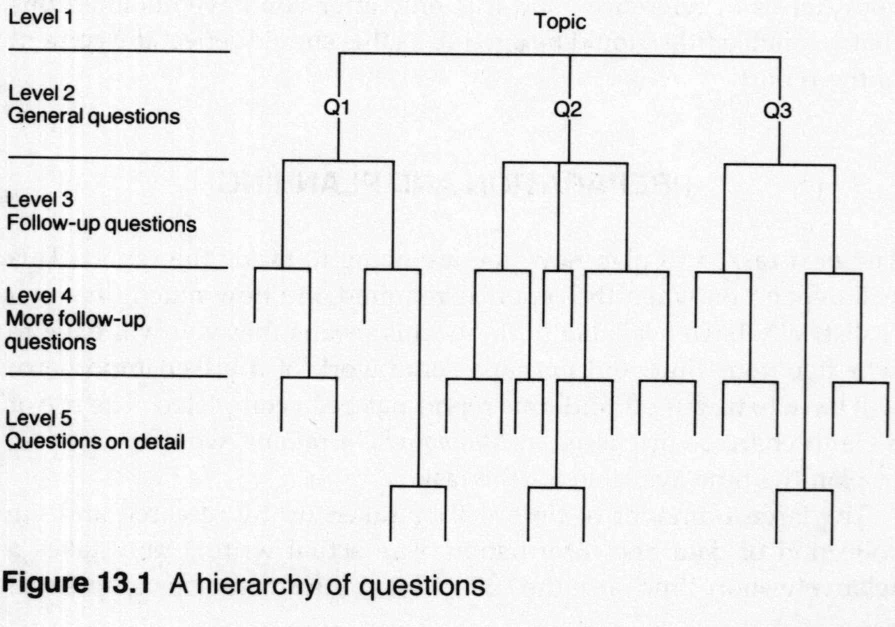

Figure 13.1 A hierarchy of questions

This sort of framework for questioning and finding information will help us to plan the final structure of the report, as the information should be in some logical order within each topic or area. Also, breaking the subject down into areas or topics and identifying the main questions will enable us to delegate some of the information gathering, wherever possible, and will enable others to help us if time is short.

After we have identified the topics or main areas and the main questions we need to answer, we will have a much better idea of how long the information gathering process will take. It may well be that some topics can be researched at the same time, while others may depend on previous research. It may well be that critical path analysis – which is covered in *Managing Operations* – would be of use here. If this shows that it is unlikely that you will be able to complete the report by the deadline, now is the time to do something about it, before it is too late.

FINDING AND COLLECTING INFORMATION

We know that very often when we are engaged in a project of some sort, ideas come to us at some unlikely times, when we are away from the work environment. We therefore need to carry a notebook and pencil to write these down before we forget them.

This includes having a notebook next to the bed for the ideas and solutions that come to us if we wake up during the night. This is not because we may then start to consciously think about the report or project but because the subconscious carries on working and does not sleep. It is therefore capable of coming up with some good ideas that we will forget by morning if we do not record them at the time.

During the fact-finding stage do be careful to obtain precise information. We have already mentioned a cost/benefit analysis, when we discussed the logical sequence of a report under Terms of Reference. Clearly a cost/benefit analysis could be a very influential means of 'selling' the recommendations of the report, and accurate figures will be necessary to achieve this. Similarly, if for example you are discussing the resiting of a department, do not simply state that the proposed area will be large enough to accommodate the unit or department. State the floor area in comparison with the present situation, comment on the need for more or less space, and quantify it. Make some diagrams with the measurements so that you can include plans and layouts in your report if you choose to.

Often you will need to be able to quote references from books and technical papers. Do make a note of the source so that you can mention it in the report or list it in the bibliography. Where you obtain opinions from key people in the company or organization, or some external expert, if a variety of opinions are offered, do be sure that you record a range of them. This will enable your report to reflect the overall views both for and against certain topics.

If you have a major project report to research and write, you may find it necessary to keep an A4 folder for each of the topics, in which to keep the data and information as you collect it. Some data as it is collected, particularly if it is in statistical form, may need calculations done on it. It will also be necessary to decide on the best format for presenting it in your report or its appendices.

When you have collected the information on each of the topics or areas you identified from your terms of reference, and any additional ones that you have since thought of, the next step is to review the quantity and quality of it.

1 Do you have enough specific information and data to write a balanced report in the depth that is required by your terms of reference?
2 Are you short of information on particular aspects?
3 Are the opinions and information verifiable? If so, from which source?
4 Is all of the information and data relevant to your subject?

If the answer to any of the above is no, then it is first necessary to go back and rectify the omission, if that is possible. If it is not possible, then it will be necessary to comment on it in your report, so that the readers can take it into account when making any decisions.

ORGANIZING AND ANALYSING

It is now time to start organizing and analysing the data and information. Obviously in the report there should be a logical flow of information which leads the reader to your conclusions and to accept your recommendations or range of options as being complete. The fact that you have carried out your research in a structured way should help you to organize the information. However, there will be links between the various topics, and some data and information will be more appropriate if moved to a different topic area.

Make a list of the conclusions that you have come to as a result of your research and check the list against your terms of reference. Then go through all of the data and information you have collected and identify all of the evidence both for and against your conclusions. This should enable you to judge whether your conclusions are based on hard evidence, or merely on 'gut feel' or personal preference. If the latter is the case, decide what further evidence is necessary, or whether you should revise your conclusions.

When you are satisfied that your conclusions fulfil your terms of reference and are supported by the facts you have collected, the next task is to identify the recommendations that you are going to make. Your report should consider several possible options, and where appropriate you should recommend a particular course of action which is supported by your findings. Much thought needs to be given to the recommendation(s), and all aspects and implications of its adoption need to be carefully considered. In particular, think how your recommendations are going to affect other people and what steps can be taken to make any adverse changes more acceptable. Think what arguments could be made against your proposals, and make a list of them and how they can be countered, or whether they in fact outweigh your views.

The next step is to decide how best you can present any statistical data so that it is most effective. The notes in chapter 8 should help with this.

WRITING THE REPORT

Writing is a form of communication and, as such, the message that is sent should be exactly the one that is received, with the minimum of effort, by the reader.

All reports need to be easily readable, and the style of writing, although personal to you, should recognize the needs of the reader. At work, most people who commission and read reports are very busy. They therefore need to be able to read and understand a report without difficulty. If their attention wanders or they need to reread sections because they are difficult to understand, it is less likely that your report will be read in its entirety or your recommendations given full consideration.

Try to write in simple English that you would use when speaking, as this will help avoid the use of 'journalese' or 'businessese'. Words like 'obviate' and 'terminate' tend only to be used in writing.

Use short words and phrases wherever possible, although some variation in this is necessary, otherwise it will become boring. All too often when writing reports people feel that they have to demonstrate the full range of their vocabulary, and as a result they use words and phrases that are unnecessarily long and complicated.

Try to avoid the use of jargon and abbreviations, as the reader can lose the train of thought whilst trying to recall what they stand for.

Do make use of charts, diagrams and illustrations wherever possible, as these can save many words.

Avoid the use of the latest management 'in' words and expressions – such as 'empowerment', 'facilitate' and 'ball park figures' – as these can irritate readers.

It must have a definite and sequential structure so that the reader is led along the 'story-line'.

STRUCTURE OF THE REPORT

1 A short report

A short report should have a beginning, a middle and an end.

The beginning comes after the title page and should contain an introduction which briefly sets out the terms of reference, the purpose and the background to the subject.

The middle or main body of the report should contain an analysis of the existing situation with advantages and disadvantages. An analysis of possible alternatives, including the facts discovered during the research, should come next. The advantages and drawbacks of each of the alternatives should be discussed with supporting evidence; sources of information and expert opinion should be quoted. The reader should be led towards your conclusions and recommendations. Any implications and implementation time-scale should be discussed here.

The final section should summarize the main findings and should state your conclusions and recommendations.

2 A long report

A report over three thousand words requires a definite structure so that readers can find their way through it and can refer to specific sections without having to reread the whole report. Some secondary readers may be requested to read certain parts of the report which are relevant to them, and a properly structured report will make it easy for them to do so.

Some companies and organizations have their own in-house structure and layout for reports, so it is necessary to check whether this applies in your company before starting.

The front cover

Many companies and organizations have their own equipment for binding reports and bulky documents. Alternatively, covers can be bought from most stationers. Some of the latter have transparent front covers so that a title page can be seen through it. Other systems will require the cover itself to have the title, author's name and department printed on it. Do remember that first impressions are very important, so large bold print is necessary.

The title page

Even if you have printed the title and your name on the cover it is still best to have a title page. This should contain the title of the report, the author's name, his or her department and location, and the date.

Acknowledgements

Where people have been particularly helpful to you in providing information or in typing the report, if it was not their job to do so, then this is the place to thank them.

The contents page(s)

The contents page lists the sections and subsections of the report by their headings and subheadings so that they can easily be referred to. Each of the sections and subsections should be allocated a numeric or alphabetic reference, and these should also be recorded against their respective headings together with the relevant page number. The contents page obviously cannot be compiled until you have completed the report and its appendices.

Terms of reference

These have been discussed earlier, and it is important to show them in full in this section of the report. This will enable anyone opening the report to see the purpose and scope and who commissioned it. It is better if the terms of reference are set out on a separate page.

Summary

This is the 'shop window' of the report and should summarize its purpose and the recommendations. This may be the only part that many people will read, and it should therefore be written to attract their attention and to interest them so that they want to read more. For some department heads, it could be that they would read the summary in order to be able to pass the report, for a more in-depth study, to someone in their department. Perhaps only part of the report will be of interest to some people, so the summary plus the contents page will be all-important in attracting their attention and directing them to the appropriate part. Obviously you cannot write the summary until you have finished the report. When you have completed it you need to review it in the same way that you would an advertisement that you had written: does it sell the report, and will it attract the attention of the people that you want it to?

Introduction

What you include in the introduction will depend very much on your potential readership. Its purpose is to put the readers in the picture as to the background of the problem and the reason for the report. If the readers are likely to include people from other organizations and/or other sites, do try to explain the background for them. This could include a description and history of your company or unit and its structure and layout etc. This will inevitably mean that your other readers who are familiar with the circumstances will skim over this part and take in the parts that are relevant to them. Include in this part a description of any limitations and assumptions that have been made, together with a list of important definitions and explanations. If the number of technical and unfamiliar words and phrases is likely to exceed four or five, it would be helpful to include a glossary of terms as the next section or as the first appendix.

Method of investigation

This section is by no means always necessary, but can be extremely helpful to readers where investigation of a technical nature has taken place. It can show the scale and depth of the research and highlight the parameters. Limitations and assumptions can be included here instead of in the summary. Any particular problems regarding the research or collection of information can also be discussed.

Main body of the report

The logical structure of this section can be all-important for the reader's understanding. A description of the present situation, even though you have already mentioned it in the introduction, is usually necessary. This should be followed by a discussion of the advantages and disadvantages of the present situation, and the need for change if this is relevant. Next should come a description of the method of carrying out the research, if a separate section on this has not already been included (see above under Method of investigation); a range of solutions or options together with a list and discussion of the advantages and disadvantages of each; the implications of each should be examined together with a cost/benefit analysis. Where the changes would affect people and jobs do make sure that you fully cover the likely implications. By the end of this section you should have included all of the information that you are going to use, as it would be wrong to introduce additional material in the conclusions or recommendations sections which follow.

Conclusions

From the information and discussions in the main body of the report, logical conclusions should now be drawn. Make sure that the order follows that of the main body and that the alternative courses of action are evaluated, as this should then lead your readers to your recommendations.

Recommendations

If you have led your readers through the main body of the report and your conclusions in a logical and structured way, then your recommendations should be obvious to them. They may not necessarily agree with all or even any of them, but they will know how you arrived at them, both with regard to the route and the information. The recommendations may also include a section on the costs saved or incurred if your proposals are implemented. An implementation plan and timescale should also be included here, if these are relevant.

Appendices

This is an area that many report writers get wrong. The appendices should be used to provide supporting evidence in the form of graphs, tables, charts, brochures, leaflets etc. which are relevant to the report. They should not be used to try to impress readers with the sheer weight of the document by putting in paper for the sake of it. All appendices should be clearly labelled and numbered so that they can be referred to in the main text and other sections, as appropriate.

Bibliography (or references)

The bibliography is a list of all of the books, magazine articles, newspaper articles, reports etc. that you have made use of or referred to in compiling your report. This will enable anyone who wants to read more on the subject to do so. Do limit this section to the important references that have played a part in or have influenced your report. Avoid the temptation of listing many others merely because you think that it will look good, as you might be expected to know something about them.

Index

In a very long report of a technical nature you might need an index to enable people to find information more easily.

LAYOUT

The appearance of the printed words on the page is important in enticing the people who open the report to read it. Small print crammed line after line on a page is very off-putting, and most of us would avoid reading it unless we had to. Also, many people who read reports like to write comments in the margins against items of interest or things that they disagree with. It is therefore necessary to have reports typed or printed in double spaced lines and with a margin of two and a half to three centimetres on both sides. Make use of headings and subheadings in bold print so that they stand out. The value of graphs, charts etc. for displaying data cannot be overstated, but do be careful to choose the most appropriate format for your purpose.

NUMBERING SYSTEMS

To enable readers to find particular passages easily and to allow you to refer to other sections, the whole of the report from start to finish needs a referencing system. In a long report it is not enough merely to number the pages, although this will usually be acceptable in a short report. In addition to page numbering, each major section (such as a chapter) will require a number with subdivisions, for different subjects, labelled with a letter or number. Further subdivisions for sections will require further letters or numbers to identify them. For example, in chapter 2 of the main body of the report, under the first subject area, the second section might be identified by the reference 2.a.(ii) or 2.1.2. The next section would then be 2.a.(iii) or 2.1.3. Very often each paragraph is numbered in one of these ways, but before you decide which one to use, check up on what the usual form is in your company or organization.

CLARITY INDEX

After you have drafted the report in full, carry out the following test on three paragraphs taken from different parts of the report.

Step 1 Count the number of words.

Step 2 Count the number of full stops and punctuation marks that replace them, such as question marks and exclamation marks, and add any colons and semicolons if you have used them.

Step 3 Divide your answer for step 1 by your answer for step 2. This will give you the 'arithmetic mean' number of words per sentence.

Step 4 Add up the number of words with more than two syllables. You need not include words that are made up of two or more words added together, like 'off-putting', or verbs the third syllable of which is an ending, as in 'dividing' or 'carrying'.

Step 5 Add the results of steps 3 and 4 together.

The lower the score achieved, the clearer the wording of the report will be and the more easily understood. You should try to keep the score below forty, and even as low as thirty if the subject is non-technical.

SUMMARY

Supervisory Management Standards:

Unit 2	Contribute to the planning, monitoring and control of resources
Element 2.1	Plan the use of resources
Element 2.2	Monitor and control the use of resources
Unit 7	Provide information and advice for action towards meeting organizational objectives
Element 7.1	Obtain, evaluate, record and store information
Element 7.2	Provide information and advice

In this chapter we looked at all aspects of writing reports.

We looked at the need for specific terms of reference to identify exactly what is required in the report, by whom and when.

We looked at planning the time for collecting and structuring the information.

The differences between the structure and requirements of short and long reports was discussed.

The style of writing was considered prior to an in-depth look at the various sections of a report.

We considered the requirements of a good layout and paragraph referencing systems.

Finally, we looked at the use of the 'clarity index' as a means of checking the readability of a report.

Chapter 14

Personal Competences

Personal competences are similar whether one is a supervisor/front line manager, a middle manager or a senior manager. The difference in how they are applied is one of dimension; all of us in supervisory and management positions need to consider how we can develop the personal competences within our work environment. A consideration of the personal competences shows that they also have a role to play in our social and domestic lives.

The personal competences most closely allied to our roles in *Managing Finance and Information* are those relating to *using intellect*. These are:

4 Using intellect to optimize results
4.1 Collecting and organizing information
4.2 Identifying and applying concepts
4.3 Taking decisions

The other personal competences are covered in the two other volumes in the *In Charge* series.

'Planning to optimize the achievement of results' is covered in *In Charge, Managing Operations*.

'Managing others to optimize results' and 'Managing oneself to optimize results' are both covered in *In Charge, Managing People*.

The Personal Competences are interrelated and in particular:

1.3, 'Monitoring and Responding to Actual Against Planned Activities', which is covered in *In Charge, Managing Operations*, can be readily applied to the section on budgets in 'Managing Finance' and the use of graphs, charts, percentages, ratios, mean, etc. which we covered in 'Managing Information'.

2.1, 'Showing Sensitivity to the Needs of Others', and 2.3, 'Obtaining the Commitment of Others', whilst fully covered in

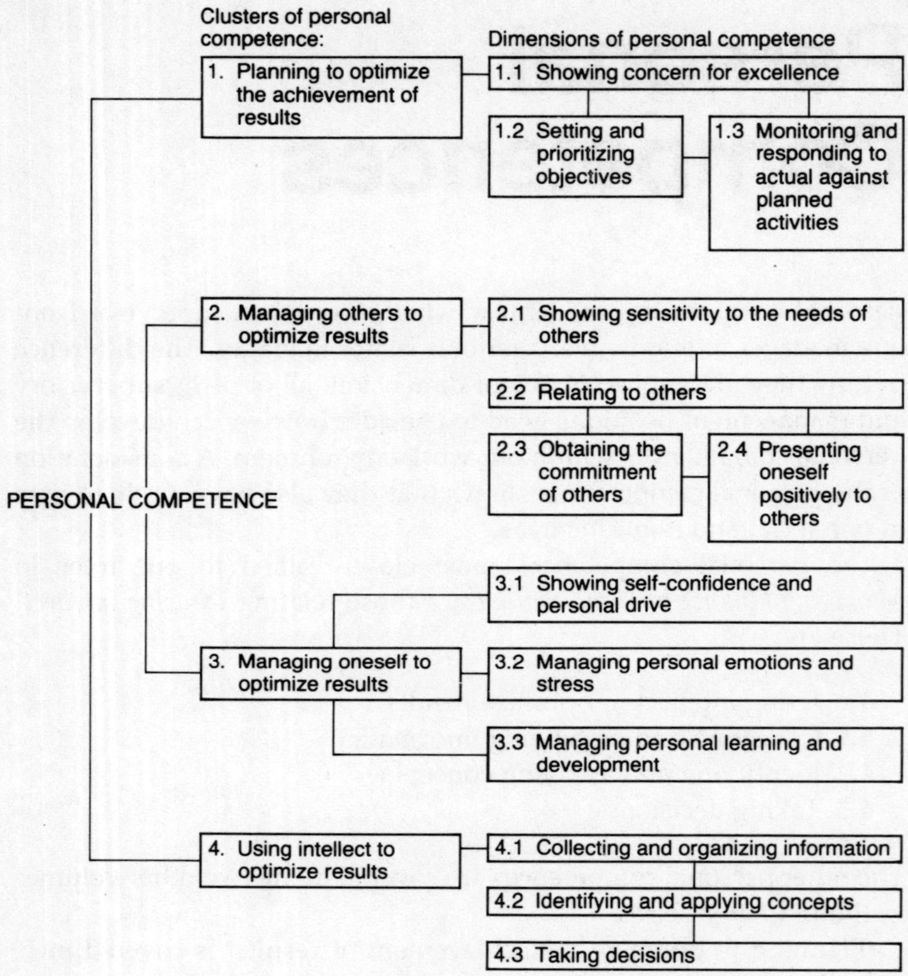

Figure 14.1 The MCI Personal Competence Model
Permission from MCI.

Managing People, can be applied to the way in which we coordinate meetings to obtain the involvement of all attendees.

2.4, 'Presenting Oneself Positively to Others', 3.1, 'Showing Self-Confidence and Personal Drive', and 3.2, 'Managing Personal Emotions and Stress', which are all covered in *Managing People*, appear to have been written regarding our feelings over interviews and making presentations, which we discussed in chapters 11 and 12.

In Charge approaches the personal competences in the form of an 'Action Plan'. When considering personal competences you should ask yourself:

- How well do I handle this area of personal competence?
- How could I handle it better?
- How does it relate to my functional competence at work?

4 USING INTELLECT TO OPTIMIZE RESULTS

Being In Charge is about getting things done through other people. The previous chapters have examined the functional competences needed to achieve the goals of the organization; personal competences are about the qualities you need to develop to achieve the best results possible. In order to do this you need to examine the ways in which you use the thinking process in your work and how you support it with information systems and other people. There are three specific areas of personal competence that are relevant to this.

4.1 Collecting and organizing information

We can regard finance as being another sort and source of information.

Every member of your department, your manager, your colleagues in other departments, your suppliers, your customers etc. are all potential sources of information. No one person can ever know everything about a department, and the need to draw on the knowledge and experience of others should be seen positively as involving others rather than as an admission of failure. No one expects you to know everything and others like to be involved.

We have already discussed how raw data is of little value until it is organized so that trends are apparent. Often raw data is destroyed because no one recognizes its potential and there is a need to be able to step back from the day-to-day business to see just what value it could have if properly collected and organized. The organization of data into the various ways of making it give up its information is something that we can practise, but we also need to give thought to its storage in terms of retrievability, access and confidentiality. We need to investigate sources of information that we might need, including making contact with people whose knowledge and experience make them 'experts'.

THINK POINT

To what extent do you believe you involve others in the collection and organization of information?

Do you have members of your unit or department who keep all knowledge and information regarding their job to themselves? If the answer is yes, what are you going to do about it?

What areas of your job do you feel that you need more information on? How are you going to develop the sources that you need?

Consider the following questions; are you satisfied that your response demonstrates your personal competence?

- Do you actively encourage free exchange of information, for example in meetings and interviews?
- Do you seek the views of others when you are analysing situations?
- If you think of a new way of doing things, do you ask to see if it has been tried before and what the result was?
- Do you gather and use all the information that is available to you from different sources?
- Do you challenge the validity and reliability of sources of information?
- Do you look to see what is missing or has been omitted from information that is given to you, either orally or in writing?
- Do you ask questions to check assumptions and to ensure quality?
- What systems, such as a personal organizer or wall chart, do you have to support your memory?

Action plan

What steps can you take to make greater use of the knowledge and experience of others? How can you improve the quality of the information you receive and use? What additional information systems do you need to set up to support you?

4.2 Identifying and applying concepts

Every job nowadays must develop as a result of new demands, new ideas, changing standards etc. This can be difficult for us, as we are programmed to resist change and may even do so without realising it. There is a need to be able to identify trends so that we can anticipate change and plan for it, rather than having to react to it when it happens. New ideas should be weighed objectively to see what improvements, if any, they can make, rather than being rejected out of hand because it is not the way we have always done things.

The people in our team and department, and our colleagues in other departments, should be encouraged to voice their ideas for improvements and know that they will receive our full consideration. We need to be able to think changes through so that we can discuss them with others, modify them where necessary, and involve others in the implementation as though it was their idea in the first place.

THINK POINT

Think of an instance when you anticipated what might happen and planned for it. What was the information that led you to identify it? What would the outcome have been if you had not anticipated it?

How often do the members of your team discuss their ideas with you for improving systems?

What were the last three occasions and what was the outcome?

When and what was the last major change you made to your job?

How entrenched are you in your routine and in your ways of doing things?

Consider the following questions; are you satisfied that your response demonstrates your personal competence?

- Can you identify patterns of meanings from factors which are not related?

- Can you convert information into another form to make it more meaningful?
- Can you distinguish cause and effect relationships in situations?
- Can you prioritize and identify key issues?
- Can you build a complete and valid picture from incomplete data?
- Can you produce your own ideas based on experience and practice 'this is what happened last time, so this time . . .'?
- Can you see situations from different perspectives?
- Do you check the logic of your own thoughts by asking others what they think?
- How well do you encourage others to put forward their ideas?

Action plan

What action do you need to take to be more receptive to new ideas and ways of working?

4.3 Taking decisions

Decision making is one of the key functions of those of us who are In Charge. Much of the quality of our decision making depends on the quality of the information on which we are basing it, so it is relevant to look at it in this section. It also depends on our attitudes and how narrow our views are; could we be accused of being blinkered?

THINK POINT

Which decisions do you take quickly and which do you delay? Try to identify the reasons for the differences.

Do you ever hold 'brainstorming' sessions with your team?

When did you last make a decision based on intuition or 'gut feel' rather than logic?

Consider the following questions; are you satisfied that your response demonstrates your personal competence?

- Are your decisions consistent with those taken in the past?
- Do you take decisions in time for them to be carried out?
- Do you make decisions that are realistic for the situation?
- Do you produce a variety of solutions before taking a decision?
- Do you make the best use of others, where appropriate, in making decisions?
- Do you balance intuition with logic in decision making?
- Can you take decisions in uncertain situations, or with incomplete information when necessary?

Action plan

What steps do you need to take to improve the quality and timeliness of your decision making?

This concludes *Managing Finance and Information*, the third volume of *In Charge: a Competence Approach to Supervisory Management*. It is a starting-point for considering the underpinning knowledge needed in these subjects by the competent supervisor/front line manager. It will not of itself make you competent: no book can do that. But it has attempted to provide you with the knowledge needed to understand the Management Charter Initiative Standards in Supervisory Management. From that knowledge, considered in respect of your work situation and past experience, can flow competence.

Glossary of Terms

This glossary contains some terms not used in *Managing Finance and Information* but likely to be met in other texts you might read.

Accrual Accounting is the accounting concept under which all income and expenditure items are taken into account when they become *due*, instead of when they are actually received or paid out. This means that we enter invoices when we receive them and not when we pay them, and we enter money due to us when we invoice our customers, not when we receive payment.

Acid Test also known as the 'Quick Ratio', indicates the ability of the company to pay its bills in a hurry if necessary. We deduct the value of its stocks from its current assets and divide the result by the total of its current liabilities.

$$\frac{\text{Quickly realizable current assets}}{\text{Current liabilities}}$$

Asset Usage Ratio measures the ability of the management to generate sales from an investment in fixed assets.

$$\frac{\text{Sales Revenue}}{\text{Fixed Assets}}$$

Assets the things a business owns. They are subdivided into fixed assets and current assets, and are defined under these headings in other parts of this glossary.

Asset Valuation assets should be valued usually at the lesser of costs or realizable value. Some fixed assets, such as land and buildings, can be professionally revalued every few years, and any surplus is added to the reserves.

Balance Sheet is a financial statement of the assets and liabilities taken at a particular point in time. It should be regarded as one frame on a cine film, as it may not be at all representative of what the business normally looks like.

Bar Charts are pictorial presentations of information where vertical or horizontal bands represent values by their height or length.

Break-even Point is the point at which the value of sales equals the total of the fixed and variable costs.

Budget is a set of mutually consistent, interrelated business plans for an organization, exhibiting quantified and feasible plans of action and forecasts of results, together with the premises on which those plans are based.

Capital is the total of the money invested in a business or borrowed for more than a short period (more than twelve months usually) to enable it to start and/or continue to operate.

Capital Employed is the total of monies invested in the business made up of shareholders' funds and loan capital.

Capital Expenditure is the money spent on fixed assets.

Cash Flow is the amount of money flowing in and out of a business, usually passing through its bank account, over a given period of time.

Cash Flow Forecast is a statement which analyses the likely money receipts and payments for a given period to anticipate any shortfalls and surpluses.

Charts information laid out in tabular form.

Contribution is the difference between sales income and the variable costs, as the resulting sum is then a 'contribution' towards the fixed costs and then to profits.

Cost Centre is that person, activity or department for which a cost may be ascertained. It is some identifiable part of the business where costs arise and where a budget can therefore be drawn up to anticipate, monitor and control those costs.

Cost Unit is a product, job, contract or unit of service for which a cost may be calculated.

Credit Period tells the management how quickly the company is getting its money in from its customers.

$$\frac{\text{Average value of debtors}}{\text{Sales revenue}} \times 365$$

Creditors are the suppliers of goods, money and services to the business which the business has not yet paid for.

Current Assets these are the things that the business owns and intends to turnover, use up, sell or convert to cash within twelve months. They include such things as raw materials, part and finished goods stocks, bank balances, debtors and cash.

Current Liabilities are debts due by the business which must be paid within a short time (less than a year usually).

Current Ratio measures the ability of a company to pay its bills.

$$= \frac{\text{Current Assets}}{\text{Current Liabilities}}$$

Data plural form of datum, which is a thing known, assumption, premise which can be used as a basis from which inferences may be drawn.

Database the computer equivalent of a store of information.

Debtors are customers who owe the business money for goods or services they have received from it.

Depreciation is the loss of value of a company's fixed assets over a period of time which results from their usage and which is charged as an expense.

Direct Costs are the costs of materials, manpower and overheads that directly relate to the production of a cost unit.

Dividends are the amounts of profit divided between the shareholders.

Equity is the amount of money due to the owners, i.e. the share capital plus reserves.

Equity Capital see *Equity*

Fixed Assets are the things the company intends to keep to use in the generation of income and in running its business.

Floppy Disk a small magnetic storage unit for programs and data for computers.

Gearing is the relationship between a company's equity capital and its loan capital.

$$\text{Gearing\%} = \frac{\text{Loan capital}}{\text{Share capital plus reserves}} \times 100$$

GIGO acronym standing for 'garbage in, garbage out'. It is used primarily with computers and indicates that the quality of the information received from the computer depends on the quality of that which was input.

Gross Profit/Loss is the sales income less the cost of the goods sold.

Histogram pictorial presentation of data similar to a bar chart, except the area of the bar is proportionate to the value of the item of data.

Investments this is money that has been placed outside the business to earn interest, dividends, capital appreciation or trading benefits (e.g., buying shares in an important supplier or customer).

Liabilities are the amounts owed to suppliers of money, goods and services to the business.

Liquid Assets are things which can be easily turned into cash. They include cash, bank balances, bills of exchange, a percentage of debtors, investments in quoted shares etc. Stock is usually excluded from liquid assets.

Liquidity Ratio see the entry under *Current Ratio*.

Loan Capital is money that has been loaned to the business on a long-term basis. The lenders usually receive an agreed rate of interest, although in the case of a small company, where the loan is from the directors, this might be nil.

Long-term Liabilities are loans, creditors etc. where the debt is not due for payment within the next year. They are shown separately in the balance sheet and details have to be given in the balance sheet notes.

Marginal Cost is the cost of producing and selling an additional cost unit.

Marginal Costing is a system whereby the variable costs are charged against cost units and the resulting contribution for that period is off-set against the fixed costs of that period.

Mean is the arithmetic average calculated by taking the sum of a series of numbers and dividing by the number of them.

Median is the value of the middle number in a series which is set out in order of values.

Microfiche is a storage system for documents on photographic film.

Mode is the most frequently appearing value in a series.

Net Current Assets is the excess of current assets over current liabilities. This is also referred to as the working capital.

Operating Profit is the profit before interest and tax are paid, and comes purely from the normal trading activities of the company.

Pictogram is a pictorial diagram used to illustrate data.

Pie Chart is a circular chart which represents the total quantity of a variable and is usually divided into segments to represent the portions of the whole.

Profit is the difference between the recorded value of a business in its books at the start of an accounting period and its increased value at the end of that period.

Profit Before Tax is the net profit of a business after the deduction of all expenses other than tax and dividends.

Profit Margin is a measure of managerial effectiveness, as it is the relationship between a company's profit before tax and interest, and its sales revenue. Because it is expressed as a percentage it reveals the amount of profit which is generated out of each pound of sales.

$$= \frac{\text{Profit before tax and interest}}{\text{Sales revenue}} \times 100$$

Quick Ratio see *Acid Test*

Ratio is a relationship between the quantities expressed in a number of units which enables comparison to be made between them.

Raw data are collections of small, individual pieces of information that are of little informational value until work has been done to sift them and to identify trends.

Reserves are made up of the profits retained in the business to provide for expansion. As such they form part of the shareholders' funds and are a part of the capital.

Retained Profits are profits retained in the business by the shareholders or with their agreement, instead of being distributed as dividends. They form part of the capital under the heading of 'Reserves' and provide for expansion of the business.

Return on Capital Employed is one of the most important ratios as a test of profitability. It measures as a percentage the profit performance before interest and tax are paid against the capital employed in the business at the start of the accounting period. This gives the amount of profit for each pound invested in the business.

$$\text{R.O.C.E.\%} = \frac{\text{Profit before tax and interest}}{\text{Capital employed}} \times 100$$

Return on Shareholders' Funds measures the rate of return shareholders have obtained on the money they have invested.

$$\text{R.O.S.F.\%} = \frac{\text{Profit after interest and tax}}{\text{Shareholders' funds}} \times 100$$

Share Capital is the money put into the business by the owners or 'shareholders' for which they receive their shares.

Software is the name given to computer programs which are not part of the machine.

Spreadsheet is a computer program which uses a grid system to display, manipulate and calculate using text, numbers, formulae and dates.

Statistics collections and classifications of numerical facts.

Stock Turnover is a measure of a company's ability to turn its finished goods into sales.

$$= \frac{\text{Sales revenue}}{\text{Stocks}}$$

Subsidiary Company is a company where 50% or more of its equity share capital is held by another company.

Tangible Assets are assets which can be touched and have a physical presence.

Trial Balance is a list of all of the balances in a business's accounts to ensure that the debit balances equal the credit balances.

Variable Costs are the costs which vary or change in line with the number of cost units produced.

Working Capital is made up of the excess of current assets over current liabilities, and is also referred to as 'Net Current Assets'.

Index